CANADA
AND
THE BRITISH IMMIGRANT

LECTOR HOUSE PUBLIC DOMAIN WORKS

CANADA
AND
THE BRITISH IMMIGRANT

EMILY POYNTON WEAVER

ISBN: 978-93-5614-601-3

Published: 1914

LECTOR HOUSE LLP
E-MAIL: info@lectorhouse.com

A FRUIT RANCH AT NELSON, BRITISH COLUMBIA

CANADA
AND
THE BRITISH IMMIGRANT

BY

EMILY P. WEAVER

Author of
"A Canadian History for Boys and Girls"
"Old Quebec: The City of Champlain" "The Story of the Counties of Ontario"
"The Trouble Man" Etc., Etc.

1914

The climate has honest heat in summer and honest cold in winter. The sun is seldom hidden, and men see many seasons, and are healthy, strong, and active.—The Marquis of Lorne, K.T.

PREFATORY NOTE

By the very writing of this book, I am in a measure offering myself as a guide to any prospective immigrant choosing to avail himself of my services. It is well, therefore, to explain that I myself came out from England, a good many years ago, as one of a large family, to settle in Canada, and so know something at first hand, of the difficulties, the trials and the pleasures that await the newcomer in the attempt to "make good" under unfamiliar circumstances.

My father had had no previous experience of farming, but fortunately one of my brothers had had a little training on a Cheshire farm. We settled ourselves on a good-sized farm in a fertile district of Ontario, and there we had an experience probably broadly resembling that of many new arrivals—sometimes amusing, sometimes vexatious, or worse. Of course we made some mistakes and had to pay for them; and we took, I am inclined to think, several years really to settle down. But in the end we all "believe in Canada," though I dare not say we believe in everything we read about Canada.

After a number of years on the farm, there followed for some of us years in Toronto and in Halifax, Nova Scotia. I may claim, moreover, to know something, still at first hand, of many parts and of all the provinces of the Dominion (save one), while it has been my lot to give for many years much time to the study of Canadian history.

The purpose of this book is, however, neither to set forth the history of the Dominion, nor to relate our own individual experiences, whilst we were "feeling our way," as a neighbour once expressed it. It is intended rather to give a general idea of the Dominion as a whole, and of each of the provinces a little more in detail, touching their history only as it seems likely to help to the understanding of what they now are, and of the attitude and ideals of the Canadian people.

I have written much of resources and opportunities, but have endeavoured also not to neglect mention of disadvantages, for Canada is no "earthly paradise," but only "a good land and a large," where there is scope for many types of human beings to develop physically, mentally and spiritually, as some of them have not room to do in the crowded centres of population in the Old World.

I should like to add that my thought always in every chapter has been of the British immigrant, present or to come; and this must be my excuse for dealing with such a familiar subject as Canada in a way that may seem to those who dwell therein to be marked both by sins of omission and of superfluity.

I have endeavoured to draw my facts and figures from reliable sources only. I have obtained them largely from government reports; but desire to acknowledge my indebtedness also to Mr. Frank Yeigh's valuable statistical compilation, "Five Thousand Facts about Canada," and to some of the special numbers of the *Globe* (Toronto) which, from time to time, publishes comprehensive reviews of conditions in the different provinces.

The black-and-white illustrations, supplementing Mr. Copping's beautiful sketches in colour, are from photographs gathered from various sources. Not a few of them, however, I owe to the courtesy of the Department of the Interior, Ottawa, the Canadian Pacific, the Canadian Northern, and the Grand Trunk Railway Companies.

Before the reader passes on to the book itself, I should like to add a word of warning. In the short interval between the writing of these pages and the revising of the proofs, conditions in Canada with regard to the demand for certain classes of labour have changed owing to the financial stringency of 1913. I believe the set-back is only temporary, and there is little probability of any decrease in the demand for men to work on the farms, for the prices of all agricultural products are high enough to warrant, if it were possible, a very largely increased output. Moreover, the harvest of the year just passed was extraordinarily bountiful and encouraging for the future.

But, for the next few months at least, persons who propose to seek work in the towns, at building and other constructive trades, or in shops or offices, would be wise to make very sure of employment in Canada, before giving up work at home. The cost of living (including house-rent, fuel, and food) is very high here; and the immigrant who arrives in slack times may have a long season of waiting for work. But he who comes out when work is plentiful is in an entirely different position, as he should be able to lay by something for a time of less general prosperity.

I would say to all prospective immigrants—*make very particular inquiries as to conditions in the special line of work you intend to follow before leaving home,* as this may save much disappointment and even hardship.

In the appendix are addresses of persons from whom further information may be obtained, notes on the government land regulations, and so forth, which it is hoped may prove of practical use to immigrants.

E. P. W.

Toronto, Ontario.
January, 1914.

CONTENTS

APPENDIX

LIST OF ILLUSTRATIONS

Page

From Drawings by Harrold Copping

CANADA AND THE BRITISH IMMIGRANT

I

WHY CANADA IS BRITISH

AFTER a pleasant voyage up the St. Lawrence, between the lines of the long French settlements on its banks, each having as its most important feature a tin-covered church spire, glinting in the sun, I remember very well coming at last through the channel between the Isle of Orleans and the northern bank to the point where, in full array, were visible the walls and towers surmounting the mighty Rock of Quebec. It was about sundown, on a glorious September evening, and the city, the river banks, and the shipping in the basin were here lit up with glowing light, there deep in warm shadow. It was in itself one of those scenes, which, for their beauty alone, fasten themselves in the memory.

But we English boys and girls, fresh from school, if we knew little else about Canada, had been thrilled by the brave story of Wolfe's victory and death on the Plains of Abraham; and so that lovely sunset scene of rock and tower, and shining water, seemed to link the history of the land we had left with the promise of the all but unknown country whither we were bound.

Never again can we see Quebec as we saw it then; yet added knowledge of its place in the story of the Empire and of Canada does not lessen its interest; and there is no spot more suitable for the telling of the reasons why it came to pass that Canada is a British land than that beneath the shadow of Cape Diamond. I am sure that the question is of interest to many a newcomer, who has preferred to emigrate to Canada, just because it is British, rather than to the United States. If, however, he has already given his attention to the subject, it will be easy to pass over this brief sketch of one phase of Canada's very interesting history to the chapters dealing more particularly with the Canada of to-day.

The name Canada, which now stands for half a continent, once belonged only to a small region, on the St. Lawrence; and at first the Canadians in general were of French race and language. A little over three hundred years ago Samuel Champlain founded Quebec, which for one hundred and fifty years was the capital of New France. Meanwhile the English colonies, which afterwards leagued themselves together to form the United States, were also growing gradually stronger through this century and a half; and almost from the beginning there was great rivalry between the French and English for the control of the eastern part of North America.

The English, neglected by their home government, and having to depend on themselves, proved the better colonizers; advancing gradually, step by step into the wilderness, and generally holding what they gained. The French, on the other hand, though excellent explorers and traders and fighters, pushed far afield, and the population of New France grew slowly compared to that of the English colonies. There was endless fighting between the representatives of the two races, both of which at times sought help from the Indians. The result was a peculiarly merciless warfare, in which women and children were murdered, prisoners tortured, and the little unprotected settlements on the frontiers constantly exposed to dreadful night attacks and the burning of their buildings and crops. The mother countries of both French and English colonists joined frequently in the struggles, and at last (as every British schoolboy knows) Quebec was taken and Canada was conquered.

But it is not so well-known by those who have made no special study of its history that the French in Canada had for years suffered sad misgovernment, many of the officials sent out from France being bent only on making money by fair means or foul. In contrast to these men, the British officers, whose duty it became, on the conquest, to govern the Canadians, seemed eminently fair and just; and the lower classes at least felt that the change was for the better. Many of the gentlemen left the country, but others remained, and the early British governors took great pains to conciliate them and the Roman Catholic priests. By the Quebec Act, which came into effect in 1775, the free exercise of the Roman Catholic religion was secured to the French Canadians as well as the retention of their old system of civil law; but in criminal cases English law was to be followed.

The Act was passed when the "Thirteen Colonies" to the south of Canada and Nova Scotia (which had become a British colony early in the eighteenth century) were on the eve of revolt, and before many months had gone by the United Colonies sent an invading army to try to force Canada to make common cause with them. But the leaders of the Canadian people proved loyal, and the invaders, though they kept up the siege of Quebec through the whole of one winter, were driven out of the country.

At that time the British inhabitants of Canada were very few, but the Revolutionary War was to do a great deal to make it strongly and positively British. Many of the people of the Thirteen Colonies were much averse from the breaking of the ties with England; and numbers of them took up arms on the royal side. When the fortunes of war went against them, many of these United Empire Loyalists were eager to leave a land which had thus cast off the old allegiance that they held dear; and the triumphant revolutionists, partly in fear of their strength, partly in hate born of the long and bitter warfare—in which both sides had been betrayed into many cruel and unjustifiable deeds—were just as eager to thrust them out.

BREAKING THE PRAIRIE BY TRACTOR AT VEGREVILLE, ALBERTA.

The British government paid vast sums in compensating the Loyalists in some measure for their losses, and in settling them in new homes. Some of them went to England; but thousands made their way to Canada and Nova Scotia, and their coming forms the best answer to the question—"Why is Canada British?"

It is British because its older English-speaking colonies were founded on the idea of "Loyalty" as some of the New England colonies were founded on a demand for religious liberty. The two colonies of New Brunswick and Upper Canada (as Ontario was named at first) owe their existence as separate provinces to the influx of Loyalists towards the close of the eighteenth century; and Lower Canada, Nova Scotia and Prince Edward Island all received large additions to their population. The number of settlers who thus came in from the former British colonies has been estimated at about 45,000.

It should not be forgotten, however, that these people, who had suffered so grievously for their adherence to their old allegiance, were not in the main blind and servile upholders of the throne for its own sake (as many of the royalists of the Stuart times had been), though unquestionably the severance of the Thirteen Colonies from Great Britain had been due in part to the efforts of George III. to become an autocratic monarch. The title bestowed on these Americans who settled in Canada—which is still a matter of pride to their descendants—was that of "United Empire Loyalists;" and always in their minds loyalty to country and empire and their ancient political institutions was associated with their loyalty to the throne.

Not a few of the leaders of the Loyalists had been men of great influence in the older colonies, and it is not surprising that almost from their arrival in what is now the Dominion of Canada, they began to agitate for representative government, and for the British institutions to which they had been accustomed. They were a liberty-loving people; and those who had settled on the St. Lawrence stoutly objected to being obliged to live under the French civil laws, which gave such satisfaction to their Gallic neighbours. They besieged the British government with petitions for a division of the Province, and for the benefit of British law; so in 1791 the old French Province was divided into Upper and Lower Canada. The newcomers thus gained the opportunity to build up a new province on British lines in the almost uninhabited western wilderness; and, having the opportunity, I think they did wonders with it.

In a hundred ways, besides the determination not to accept any limitation of their political liberty, they showed their force and energy of character. The task that faced Canada's first British pioneers was more strenuous than that which has faced any pioneers since, though the opening and subduing of a new land to the uses of civilized man is always a task that tests to the utmost the manhood and womanhood of those who essay it.

The land was thickly covered with huge trees, and in many places the soil, which the sun's rays could scarcely ever reach through the shadowy verdure of the woods, was cold and wet and swampy. When the Loyalists came, there were no roads in Upper Canada or New Brunswick. There were no steamboats on the lakes or rivers, no railroads even dreamed of. The monarchs of the forest appeared to those first settlers in the light of enemies, to be put out of the way by axe and fire as speedily as possible, and in many districts the land was savagely stripped bare of woods, in a fashion that those who have come after cannot help regretting. It was only the ashes of the majestic maples and beeches and walnuts which had any value in the eyes of the pioneers. Made into potash these would fetch a little ready money, hardly to be obtained in those early days for any other commodity. Even for wheat, only "store-pay" could usually be obtained, and but a small allowance of that, for the great world's markets were utterly inaccessible to Canada's early farmers, and the local demand was very small.

It was the age of home industries, when every man was by turns builder of his own log-house; cabinet-maker of such rude attempts at chairs and tables as he could turn out; farmer of patches of grain amongst the slowly rotting stumps of forest trees; roadmaker, of ways "slashed" through the bush and stretches of corduroy over the swamps.

Meanwhile his wife was not only dressmaker, but spinner and weaver of stout "homespun"; not only housekeeper, but maker of candles and soap; not only cook of the daily meals, but baker of bread, when flour could be got, and contriver of some substitute for it when pounded maize or Indian meal had to be used instead.

And these lists might be extended indefinitely. The people drank tea made from a wild plant growing along the edges of the swamps, and sweetened it with sugar made by boiling the sap drawn in the spring from their own maple trees. Such articles as spoons were cut from bass wood. Shoes were fashioned by the father of the family from the skins of the animals he killed. The arrival, or the making, of the first wheeled vehicle in some settlements was an event, the only kind of conveyance used at first being a rude "sled" drawn by oxen.

Chapters might be written on the means by which the Loyalists came to Canada. Often their journeys from their old homes took weeks. Many came by sea from New York to the Maritime Provinces, and a piteous sight they presented, on their arrival, in worn and often positively ragged clothing. Others came in canoes or heavier wooden boats, making long roundabout voyages up one stream and down another to Lake Ontario, but in places having to carry both boats and goods across a long "portage." Yet others, of the more fortunate class, who had saved something from the wreck of their fortunes, travelled in big covered wagons, which served for tents at night for the women and children; and some brought in a cow or two as well as the horses or oxen that drew their vehicles.

Many of the Loyalists had lost all, and depended for their new start in life entirely on the bounty of the government. Others had some means of subsistence left, not a few having served as officers during the Revolutionary War and drawing half-pay. They were of all classes, from ex-officials of the revolted colonies, clergymen, doctors, lawyers, and merchants to private soldiers, labourers, Indians and even negro slaves.

Many of them were men and women of good education, and one of the most difficult problems to be faced in the new settlements was the education of the children. Soon many tiny log school-houses were put up, and the demand for teachers was so great that anyone who had a smattering of knowledge had a good chance to be put in charge of a little school. Often, however, it fell to the mother to give her boys and girls their first lessons in reading and writing by the hot light of the great fires that roared up the chimneys on a winter's evening.

Books in the settlements were few, but generally well read, newspapers were non-existent, and there are traditions in more than one settlement of an obliging postmaster, who used to carry the whole "mail" of a district about with him in his hat, so that he might distribute the letters as occasion offered.

Amongst these pioneers laboured missionaries of different denominations, whose experience of toilsome journeys and perils by land and water resembled those of the Apostles. In canoes, on foot or on horseback they tried courageously to serve the needs of parishes that are now counties; and great was the rejoicing when at last some little log-church was built, though it might have no seats but rough boards set on short pieces of tree trunks.

In these years of hardship the courageous spirit and the useful experience of the Loyalists triumphed, and well and truly did they lay the foundation of a new British nation in the north. Some Americans of adventurous turn of mind, but not of their political creed, early found their way into the land; but when in June, 1812, there broke out between the young American Republic and England a war, which had grown out of the struggle of the last-named nation with Napoleon, it was the old spirit of the Loyalists which dominated Canada; and in a long three years' conflict they again and again beat back the invaders across their frontiers. They were indeed well aided by the French of Lower Canada, and by newcomers from the British Isles; but, whoever might falter, the Loyalists were determined that their new country should remain British.

This, of course, tended to draw other immigrants loyal to the Empire to Canada. Of these later immigrants something will be said in dealing with the separate provinces; but Canada as a whole has never lost her heritage of loyalty, nor of the independence of spirit which has come to her from the descendants of the men who forced the Great Charter from the reluctant tyrant John, and of those who extorted the assent of King Charles to the Bill of Rights.

As the years went on, it was found difficult in practice to evolve a system by which the new British-American colonies should have the full liberty they demanded without weakening the tie binding them to the Mother-land. When Upper and Lower Canada were separated, Lieutenant-Governor Simcoe congratulated the former province on possessing a "transcript of the British constitution," but the measure of self-government given was much less than that which the men of the British Isles had attained; and there was difficulty and blundering and heart burning, there was even an actual rebellion in the Canadas before a really satisfactory system of colonial government was worked out.

QUEBEC FROM THE CHÂTEAU FRONTENAC.

It is interesting that, to a large extent, the political institutions of Canada, like those of the Mother-land, are not what might be described as an invention of any statesman, or group of statesmen, but rather resemble a living organism, which, in order to survive and grow, has had to adapt itself to its environment. At first, after the rude shock of the secession from the Empire of the Thirteen Colonies, British statesmen were nervously apprehensive that the growth of the new colonies in wealth and power would inevitably result in their separation from Britain. Then there arose a school of statesmen, who were prepared to acquiesce with eagerness in any step on the part of the "overseas dominions" in the direction of independence. But after more than a century of dangers and vicissitudes the Canadian provinces are British still; and the politicians in England who wish to bid them farewell are no longer numerous.

That they are British (to return to the point whence we started) is due above all to the sturdy spirit of the brave old Loyalists who formed the earliest large accession of British immigrants to Canada. They had their faults; they were not free from the bitterness and cruelty with which they charged their victorious opponents. They were martyrs of a lost cause, and as a class were never remarkably patient sufferers; but they were undoubtedly fine material for the building of a new nation, and the debt that Canada owes to them is not to be lightly estimated.

When it appeared (as it soon did appear) that the form of representative government granted to the colonies was only a shadow of the popular government of the Mother-land, the liberty-loving colonists began a persistent and long-continued agitation for a change. The flaws in the colonial form of government were that at first the representatives of the people had no control over the finances of the several provinces; and that the government was administered by the officials of what was called the "Executive Council," who were appointed, and could only be removed, by the royal governor representing the Crown, and were not in any way responsible to the electors of the colonial Assemblies. The executive councillors were in a position to bid defiance to the popular branch, especially as the Legislative Council, or Upper House, of the colonial legislatures, composed of men appointed by the governor, usually made common cause with them against the Assemblies. In fact, in the Canadas many men had seats in both councils; and in Nova Scotia and New Brunswick one council had both legislative and executive functions.

After a short period, even the governors sent out from England were at a great disadvantage compared with the councillors, many of whom had spent the greater part of their lives in the colony. A newly-arrived governor naturally looked to his councillors for advice and information. It was they and their families who formed the most important part of his little court, and if he did not speedily fall under their influence, he had many difficulties thrown in his way. In Lower Canada the political troubles were aggravated by the fact that almost all the members of the legislature and Executive Councils belonged to the small English-speaking Protestant minority.

For nearly half a century the disputes between the different branches of the government continued; but at last, after the rebellion of 1837-38, Lord Durham was sent as High Commissioner to Canada, and though his conduct of affairs was severely criticized at home, he managed to probe to the bottom the chronic state of discontent in the colonies; and the remedy he recommended was that the executive in the colonies should be made, as in England, responsible to the people, and that the body of officials in the several provinces should only continue to rule while they could command the support of a majority in the Assemblies. His advice was followed, and within a few years all the provinces had "Responsible Government."

Thus was forged another link which bound the colonies to the Empire, for at last the people felt that the Mother-land could no longer be blamed for any blunders and wrong-doing in the administration of the governments on this side of the ocean; and the electors knew that if the government was not so good as it might be, it was at least as good as those who put it into power deserved to have. The system had also, like its British model, a flexibility and a capacity for readjustment to new situations or more advanced views, which made it peculiarly suited to a land where conditions are constantly changing.

The government has remained to this day essentially British in its underlying principle of the ultimate responsibility of the cabinet to the electors, though in some respects, since the confederation of the provinces, it has had in outward appearance a considerable resemblance to the government of the United States.

II

THE DOMINION OF CANADA

HISTORICALLY, the Dominion of Canada was evolved from the separate provinces; but it will be more convenient here to consider it as a whole before giving some account of each of the nine provinces separately. In this chapter, and generally throughout the book, when I speak of Canada, I mean the Dominion of Canada, though the name was first applied to the French province on the St. Lawrence, which was sometimes also called New France. Afterwards, for three-quarters of a century, from 1791 to 1867, the province now known as Quebec was called Lower Canada, or Canada East; and that now known as Ontario, Upper Canada, or Canada West.

The immense area of Canada is one of its most striking features. Its size is one of the reasons that it is a land of great opportunity; it is also the root of many of the most difficult problems of its government and development. In area it is over 3½ million square miles; that is to say, it is a little larger than the United States, or than Europe would be without France. It stretches from the Atlantic Ocean on the east to the Pacific on the west, and from the United States boundary on the south to the Arctic Ocean on the north. The distance from Halifax in Nova Scotia to Vancouver in British Columbia is about 3,660 miles, whilst that from Halifax to Liverpool is only about 2,820; and the traveller, wishing to go from Victoria in Vancouver Island to Dawson in the Yukon District, has to make a journey by land and water of over 1,500 miles.

It is just as well for the intending immigrant to try to realize that Canada is a land of "magnificent distances"; otherwise, on his outward journey, perhaps to some point in the far west, it may seem that the distance he is putting between himself and his old home is interminable. With modern conveniences of travel, however, the immigrant of to-day can come from England and cross Canada to Vancouver in a shorter time than it took the Loyalists to go from New York to Toronto.

The most southern point of Canada, a little islet in Lake Erie, is only about the same distance from the equator as is Valladolid in Spain, whilst Toronto is in nearly the same latitude as Florence, and the new town of Prince Rupert, far up on the Pacific seaboard of the Dominion, is not much farther north than Liverpool.

The vast extent of country and the variety in its physical features cause considerable differences of climate; but generally the interior is rather colder than the same latitudes in the west of Europe, and the summer, though hot and dry, is shorter than in Europe. The climate in the region near the Atlantic is colder than the countries on the opposite side of that ocean, owing to a cold current which flows southward along its shores from the Arctic regions; but the Pacific Coast, which has the benefit of the warm Japanese current, has a climate very much resembling that of the British Isles.

Upon the whole, however, it may be said that one of the strongest points of the Canadian climate generally is its amount of sunshine and clear weather. Even in the high latitudes the summer, though short, is warm, and, of course, as one goes further north, the possible number of hours of sunshine in the day during the summer increases, so that growth is extremely rapid. Thus results the ripening of crops of grain and vegetables and certain kinds of fruit much farther north than a mere glance at the map would lead one to expect. There has as yet been little systematic experiment as to what crops can be grown in the higher latitudes; but for generations vegetables have been cultivated in the gardens of the Hudson's Bay Company's factors, and also at many a mission station in the northern wilderness; and it is an interesting circumstance that the imaginary line beyond which profitable farming has been supposed impossible has again and again been pushed farther north.

Till within the last half century, indeed, the "North-West Territories" were held by the Hudson's Bay Company, and as agriculture and fur trading are hardly compatible industries, it was not to the interest of this powerful fur trading corporation to advertise the agricultural possibilities of the country, nor to set right the popular misconception of British North America as a land of nothing but snow and ice. It is quite true that it has snow and ice in plenty; but there is a golden side to the shield as well as a silver one; and Canada might just as fairly claim the title of "Our Lady of the Sun" as that of "Our Lady of the Snows."

A feature of the Dominion, of which the ordinary small-scale map gives little idea, is the diversity of surface. Every map indeed suggests in the west the bold line of the Rocky Mountains, but even in that case scarcely hints at the fact that between the Pacific Ocean and the prairie regions, the mountain barrier is ranged rank behind rank, peak above peak.

In the ordinary map, moreover, the eastern provinces look as level as the prairies; but they are not so. The Maritime Provinces, Quebec and Ontario, may be described generally as a land of plains and valleys and hills, which, in some regions, rise to an elevation deserving the name of mountains—a word which is used somewhat freely in Canada.

The map usually does make clear to a careful student of it the fact that the Dominion upon the whole is a land of noble rivers and of lakes, some small, some large enough to deserve the name of inland seas, though they have neither the salt of the sea nor its tides; and that Canada does actually possess one great inland sea, a thousand miles long and six hundred miles broad, in Hudson Bay. This thrusts itself deep into the heart of the country, and for a couple of centuries was, as it may soon be again, a recognized gateway to the interior.

Of course, altitude and "the general lie of the land" have a great influence on climate as well as latitude. The prairie country is more correctly a series of plateaux than a great plain; and though one hardly realizes the fact when travelling across it, there is a great difference of level between the region about Winnipeg, and that where it approaches the foot hills of the Rocky Mountains. The altitude of Winnipeg is only seven hundred and fifty-seven feet above the sea-level, whilst that of Calgary is actually two hundred feet higher than the topmost peak of Sea Fell, England's highest mountain; and perhaps the elevation of much of the country accounts not only for its being colder than some corresponding latitudes of the old world, but also for the buoyant atmosphere in the west, and for the characteristic hopefulness and eagerness and energy of the people.

A great part of northern Canada is still a wilderness, only partially explored; and at brief intervals comes news from east or west or north of some fresh discovery of minerals or water powers; or amazingly fertile soil, in some region where no one had dreamed hitherto of reaping a harvest.

This kind of thing gives a curious interest to life in Canada. No doubt it is akin (on a smaller scale) to the spirit of expectancy and readiness for adventure which reigned in Europe in the years immediately following the discovery of America.

But it has been proved over and over again that the gifts of the wilderness are only to be won at great cost of toil, and struggle, and loneliness; and few men or women are cut out for the *rôle* of pioneer. In Canada hundreds of people every year venture to undertake tasks for which they are not fitted either by knowledge or previous experience or natural tastes, and the result is a vast amount of unnecessary suffering and disappointment, and often loss of health and even life; but I shall have more to say on this matter when dealing with the subject of the opportunities for immigrants. Here I would only add that there are numerous openings for people willing to work in the more settled communities as well as on the very frontiers of civilization; and that Canada has a great variety of opportunities to offer on easier conditions than actual pioneering.

If any one is attempting to obtain a true idea of the resources and opportunities of the Dominion, he should be very particular to bear in mind exactly what part of the country his informant is discussing. It is so large a country that persons talking loosely of what there is or is not "in Canada," though their remarks may be perfectly accurate with regard to one district, may be totally misleading with regard to another. For example, in the Eastern Provinces, ivy and holly and broom are never seen growing in the open air, though the first-mentioned plant is often grown in pots as a house plant; but in Vancouver and Victoria ivy-covered buildings are as common as in England, and so are hedges and bushes of glossy holly. It is the same in matters other than vegetation. There are differences of manner and custom in different localities. French Canada is a quaint old-world land—how old-world the visitor must penetrate into the country to discover. But the "habitants," speaking their French patois, scarcely differ more in many of their characteristics from the "go-ahead" English-speaking "Westerners" and the stalwart Nova Scotian fishermen, than do these two latter types differ from each other. You may find that your copper coins will not pass current in a new prairie town, but even a little further east a "cent" will buy a few things, including an enormous morning newspaper, excepting on the train.

1. BREAKING THE PRAIRIE WITH OXEN, THUNDER HILL DISTRICT.

2. TRANSPORTATION IN THE WEST: SETTING OUT FOR THE NEW HOME WITH OXEN IN THE WEST.

It is not indeed surprising that there are many cases in which you cannot judge fairly or accurately of one place by another two thousand miles or more distant, even if both happen to be in Canada. Perhaps, indeed, one of the most general characteristics of the country is what some people might call its incongruities. Take a few instances at random. Canada has cities, where its richer folk live in luxury, and its poorest inhabit genuine slums (more's the pity). It has, too, small villages and backwoods settlements and country communities, where class distinctions are of little account. In some towns you may see a smart up-to-date motor car, cheek by jowl with an ox wagon. It has a goodly list of well-equipped hospitals, but there are many remote settlements where a doctor is hardly to be had in direst emergency for love or money.

The observation that is true in some well-settled districts may not hold in the depth of its unbroken unexplored woods. One may know "Canada" as a land of quiet hills and valleys, but perhaps the name stands to his brother for a "sea of mountains," with hundreds of "unconquered peaks" luring the Alpine climber to triumph or disaster. It may be that your Canada is the wide, open prairie country far inland, beautiful in its season, with a wealth of bright flowers or square miles of waving wheat; while the name for me means a rugged coast, where the great Atlantic rollers beat on cliffs of granite, or toss the white-sailed fishing boats in too-rough jest or fury.

"Canada" means all these things and many more. Its life is too complex, its resources too various to be presented satisfactorily in a single sketch; and yet behind all diversity the name does stand for a real unity and a growing national consciousness.

III
CONFEDERATION

NOW and for many a year past the whole vast country has been under one government, and this is a fact that is of a good deal of importance outside merely political circles. Unlike the Federal Government of its great neighbour, the several states of which united to resist pressure from the mother country without, "Confederation" in the case of the Dominion resulted largely from troubles within the provinces.

After the rebellion of 1837-38, the two provinces of Upper and Lower Canada were united under one government, with one legislature in which, though the population of the latter province was considerably larger than that of the former, each province was represented in the House of Assembly by forty-two members elected by the people, and in the Legislative Council by ten councillors appointed for life by the governor. The French naturally objected to this arrangement. They also objected to the assumption by the new province of the debts of both older ones, when the debt of Lower Canada was much smaller than that of Upper Canada; for, though part of the debt of the latter had been incurred in making canals and other improvements likely to be of advantage to the country generally, the French Canadians had, of course, never been consulted about the spending of the money.

In process of time, however, the relative position of the uneasily-yoked-together provinces altered.

In 1853 a bill was brought in, increasing the number of members of the Assembly from forty-two for each province to sixty-five. By this time the population of Upper Canada had outstripped that of the Lower Province, and there arose a demand amongst the English-speaking people for representation in proportion to population.

It is not surprising that the French Canadians, who had at first been the party to suffer by the forced equality of membership, resented and resisted the agitation for "Rep. by Pop.," as it was often called. At that time it seemed as if the long-desired boon of responsible government were going to prove a failure in Canada, for the representatives of the people were split up into so many different groups—French and English; Reformers and Conservatives, both moderate and extreme, none of whom could arrive at any means of working harmoniously together. Any one of the numerous parties, standing alone, was sure to be outvoted; and it sometimes happened that opponents would unite to drive a third party from power, but not to give strength to any government.

The rivalry between the representatives of the French and English provinces was most dangerous to the principle of responsible government, for it could, and did happen, that measures affecting only one of the provinces were forced upon it by a majority drawn chiefly from the other province; and this caused very bitter and angry feeling. For instance, in this way a number of separate public schools for the Roman Catholics were firmly established in Upper Canada. Some people asserted, therefore, that it was the duty of a government to resign office if outvoted on a particular measure by the representatives of the province chiefly concerned, even though the majority of the whole House might be with it.

Another grave difficulty was that it led to grievous waste of the public money, for if money were voted for some public work in one province, an equal amount, whether needed or not, was usually voted for the other. These complications absolutely paralysed the working of the system of Party Responsible Government. Ministers rose and fell; dissolution of parliament succeeded dissolution; but there was no sign of any end to the confusion.

In different parts of British North America the plan of a Confederation of the Provinces, with one central government to control matters common to all, and provincial legislatures to manage local affairs, was advocated from time to time. The Maritime Provinces of Nova Scotia, New Brunswick, and Prince Edward Island had their own problems and difficulties, and in 1864 their statesmen agreed to meet at Charlottetown, in Prince Edward Island, to discuss the question of a union amongst themselves.

By that time affairs in United Canada (was there ever a greater misnomer?) had reached a positive deadlock. At the beginning of the year, in succession to a reform ministry, which had only weathered the political tempests for a few months, Sir Etienne Taché and Mr. (afterwards Sir) John A. Macdonald had formed a Conservative government. Even at first they had a bare majority and presently they were outvoted by a majority so narrow that there was not any reasonable ground for hope that if they resigned, their opponents would be less helpless, or that if parliament were dissolved parties would be less evenly balanced. A dissolution seemed inevitable, however, when there arose a sudden light in the darkness.

George Brown, the leader of the English-speaking reformers, came to the rescue and promised the support of himself and his party to the ministers, if they would seriously set themselves to find a way out of the difficulty. Macdonald and his coadjutors met their old opponents half way. A coalition government was formed, and it was decided to try to form a federal, in place of a legislative, union, including all the provinces or the two Canadas alone. It is needless here to dwell on the delays and difficulties with which the project was beset. In October, 1864, representatives of Upper and Lower Canada, and of the Maritime Provinces, including Newfoundland, met at Quebec to formulate a scheme of confederation; but neither of the two island provinces made part of the Dominion of Canada, as it commenced its existence on July 1, 1867. Prince Edward Island came into the union six years later; but Newfoundland stands aloof to this day.

The British North America Act of the Imperial parliament, which finally gave effect to the desire of the provinces for union, embodied, with little alteration, the scheme agreed upon at Quebec in 1864. The act provided for the admission into confederation of other provinces besides the original four, and, as has already been mentioned, the Dominion of Canada now consists of nine provinces besides some large tracts of unorganized and sparsely populated territory in the north.

The Dominion parliament has power to make laws for "the peace, order and good government of Canada," except with regard to certain matters put under the jurisdiction of the provincial legislatures. The parliament consists of the King (represented by the Governor-General), an Upper House, or Senate, and a Lower House, or House of Commons.

The Senate consists of eighty-three members, who are appointed for life by the Governor-in-Council, but no man who is under thirty years of age, or not by birth or naturalization a British subject, is eligible for appointment. He must also be possessed of real or personal property worth $4,000 (£800), and must be, and continue to be, a resident of the province for which he is appointed.

The House of Commons consists (at present) of two hundred and fourteen members, elected with regard to a fair representation of the relative population of the different sections of the country by the following plan:—The province of Quebec has always sixty-five members, and the other provinces have a number of members bearing the same proportion to their populations as sixty-five bears to the population of Quebec. The representation is adjusted after every decennial census—the last census being taken in 1911. The population of the West naturally increases much faster than that of the older provinces, and consequently every census requires a readjustment in favour of the West. For instance, during the decade following the census of 1891, Ontario had ninety-two members and Manitoba had only seven, but since 1901 the number of Ontario's members has dropped to eighty-six, while that of Manitoba has risen to ten, and the next readjustment, which is already overdue, will show an even greater change in the balance of population.

In the Dominion, as in the provincial parliaments, the principle followed is that of responsible cabinet government; and in this important respect it resembles the British system, and differs from the government of the United States. In the latter country, the appointment of all the chief executive officers rests with the President, subject to the consent of the Senate. Thus, as Professor Goldwin Smith puts it, "instead of a ministry responsible to the legislature and dependent for existence on its vote, America has a ministry independent of the legislature and irremovable during its term of four years." But, in Canada, when a man takes office in the ministry he must go back to his constituents for re-election; and though the normal life of the House of Commons is five years, it may be dissolved at any time by the Governor-General on the advice of his ministers. Of course, if a cabinet is defeated it must resign and give place to one which has the confidence of the House. In this way, the will of the people (or it would be more correct to say of the men, for women have as yet no voice in the election of members to parliament) is supreme in Canada; and they must, in the last resort, hold themselves responsible for the doings of the men whom they put or retain in office.

THE HOUSES OF PARLIAMENT, OTTAWA.

The qualifications entitling persons to vote are the same with regard to the Dominion House of Commons and the provincial legislatures. Women are excluded from voting on any but municipal elections, and males must be of the age of twenty-one years and be British citizens by birth or naturalization. In Ontario, Manitoba, Saskatchewan, Alberta and British Columbia the vote is given after a term of residence varying from six to twelve months (practically to every adult male citizen, though he may be utterly illiterate and ignorant of either the English or French tongues). In the Maritime Provinces even an adult male citizen cannot vote, unless he has been resident for twelve months in the province, and has qualifications "based" on ownership of real property, position as teacher or clergyman, personal property or income. The same applies to Quebec, except that in that province the would-be voter may qualify in one month's residence.

By the British North America Act, the Dominion parliament has control of all matters not specially assigned to the provincial legislatures. This is another respect in which the Canadian constitution differs from that of the United States, where "the residuum of power" was retained by the States which entered into the Federal Union. In other words, in the United States all matters not specially put under the jurisdiction of the central authority remain to be dealt with by the individual states; while in Canada the authority of the Dominion parliament extends to all affairs not specially reserved to the jurisdiction of the provinces.

In general terms, the Dominion parliament has power to make laws regarding affairs that concern all the provinces, but a number of matters are specially enumerated as being within the jurisdiction of the central government. These are as follows:—Public debt and property; trade and commerce; taxation (any system) and the borrowing of money on the public credit; the postal service; the census and statistics; militia, military and naval service and defence; the fixing of salaries for government officers; lighthouses and coast service; navigation and shipping; fisheries; quarantine; currency and banking; weights and measures; interest; legal tender; bankruptcy, and the general financial and commercial system; patents and copyrights; Indians and reserves for Indians; naturalization; marriage and divorce; the criminal law and penitentiaries; the territories not within the boundaries of any province and the establishment of new provinces.

The matters put under the control of the provinces are:—The amendment of the provincial constitutions (except as to the lieutenant-governor); direct taxation and borrowing of money on the provincial credit for provincial purposes; provincial officials; management and sale of provincial public lands and forests; regulation of asylums, hospitals, charities, reformatories and jails; municipal institutions; shop, tavern and other licences; solemnization of marriage; property and civil rights; constitution and maintenance of provincial courts of civil and criminal jurisdiction; the appointment of magistrates and justices of the peace; education, with certain exceptions as to the separate schools of religious minorities; and local works and matters of a merely private nature in a province.

With regard to immigration and agriculture, both Dominion and provincial parliaments may legislate, but in case of conflicting legislation the Dominion Act overrules the provincial. The Governor-in-Council of the Dominion may disallow an Act of a provincial parliament, within one year of its passing, and the Imperial government in like manner may disallow an Act passed by the Dominion parliament within two years after its receipt by the Secretary of State for the Colonies; but the power of disallowance is used very rarely. If an Act passed by the Dominion or a provincial parliament exceeds, as sometimes happens, the powers given under the British North America Act, the courts may declare it *ultra vires*—that is, "beyond the powers" of the legislature which enacted it. The provinces may neither organize nor maintain a provincial military force; and here again the constitution of Canada differs from that of the United States, under which each State may have a military force.

The revenue of the Dominion is obtained from taxation (largely in the form of duties on imported goods), "from receipts from the sales of the crown lands, from the post office, from railways, canals and other sources." Upon their entrance into confederation each of the provinces resigned its right to levy indirect taxes; and in place of this each province receives a subsidy from the Dominion.

The Dominion at the time of Confederation took over the public debts of the several provinces; and further debts have been incurred in the building of canals, railways, and other public works. To set against these the Dominion possesses immensely valuable assets in her millions of acres of ungranted lands and in her state-owned railways, canals, and public buildings for various purposes.

Since Confederation the provinces have also incurred public debts, largely in constructing works to improve communication, and in the erection of public buildings.

The capital of the Dominion is the city of Ottawa, beautifully situated on the right bank, or Ontario side, of the Ottawa river, which forms a considerable part of the boundary between the provinces of Quebec and Ontario.

Ottawa was founded by a gallant English officer, Colonel John By, after whom the original little village built at the point where the Rideau river falls into the Ottawa, was called Bytown. The name—quaintly suggestive of the *Pilgrim's Progress*—would not have been as euphonious a title for the metropolis of the Dominion as is Ottawa; but one cannot help regretting that this tribute to By should have been swept from the map, for he certainly deserves remembrance. He came to Canada in 1802, when he had just reached manhood, and was stationed for nine years in the picturesque old capital of Quebec. He was recalled to serve in the Peninsular war, but in the spring of 1826 received orders to go again to Canada to superintend the construction of the Rideau canal. The experiences of the war of 1812 had made the authorities desirous to open another route for the transportation of troops and supplies to the upper country than that by the St. Lawrence, which was much at the mercy of the Americans, and so it was decided to construct a system of canals and dams and locks to connect and improve the natural waterways and give communication between the Ottawa river and Kingston on Lake Ontario.

The task was a difficult one. The country was then scarcely inhabited, and the work had to be carried through tracts of swamp and morass, where the surveyors and workmen frequently contracted fever and ague; but By refused to be discouraged. For six years his stalwart, soldierly figure, often mounted on a coal-black charger, was a familiar sight in the mushroom village which sprang up on the southern bank of the Ottawa or Grand river.

Besides civilian workmen, he had at his command a company of sappers and miners, a fact recalled to-day by the name of the "Sappers' Bridge" at Ottawa; and traditions still linger of his perseverance, his determination to accept no scamped work, and his kindness of heart. One all but completed dam went down before an ice-jam, and a new bridge was swept away by a spring flood; but the indomitable colonel took these disasters merely as a challenge to build more strongly, and at last the whole waterway, one hundred and twenty-six miles in length, with its twenty-four dams and its forty-seven locks, was open for navigation.

In the same year the colonel was called home, not to receive praise and honour for his achievement, but to serve, it has been said, as "a scapegoat" for the government, which had been attacked for spending public moneys without the authority of parliament. The blow was crushing, and falling into "low spirits," the gallant gentleman could no longer triumph over misfortunes, but died a few months later in his fifty-third year.

But Bytown prospered. Till the St. Lawrence canals were completed the whole trade between Upper and Lower Canada passed through the rough little village, and to visitors it seemed that Bytown folk were too busy to pave their streets or to think of gardens or flowers. The Upper and Lower towns on either side of the hill, then crowned by the barracks, now by the parliament buildings, were separate villages. Then, as now, it was a great lumbering centre, and there were wild doings when gangs of lumber-jacks came down from the woods for business or pleasure. Whiskey was deplorably cheap, and the woodsmen often fought savagely amongst themselves, or with the Irish "shiners" who rafted the lumber down the river; and sometimes they made "felonious assault" on unoffending citizens. But despite the rude accompaniments of the lumber trade, it was building up Bytown, which was incorporated as a town with six thousand inhabitants fifteen years after the completion of the Rideau canal. Eight years later it became a city, and changed its name to Ottawa.

In the fifties, there was an inconvenient arrangement, by which the cities of Toronto and Quebec served alternately for four years each as capital of Upper and Lower Canada (then united), but in 1857 Queen Victoria was asked to name a permanent capital. On account of its central position with regard to the two provinces, its distance from the international boundary line; and above all, perhaps, because of descriptions which she had heard of the striking beauty of its site, Her Majesty made choice of Ottawa. The erection of the beautiful parliament buildings was soon afterwards begun, and at Confederation the city became the capital of the Dominion, whilst the rank of provincial capital was restored to the larger city of Toronto.

Ottawa, with its suburbs, now has about one hundred and twenty-five thousand people and its chief interests are still lumber and legislation. A little army of its breadwinners finds employment, in some capacity or other, in connection with the business of government. Each of the departments of state has, of course, a large staff, from experts of various descriptions down to clerks and office boys.

The official residence of the Governor-General is Rideau Hall. This long, low, rambling erection is hardly picturesque, though it is decidedly old-fashioned. It stands in pleasant grounds, and its nucleus, "the Castle," as it was called, was built in 1838, by a Scottish member of parliament, named McKay. The original house had a score of rooms, but the present-day Hall has over a hundred, which have been added from time to time to suit the convenience of its noble occupants. For instance, the great ballroom dates from Lord Dufferin's time; while the racquet court was built by the Marquis of Lorne, a studio by the artistic Marchioness, and the chapel by the Earl of Aberdeen.

Other places at Ottawa of national interest, either for what they are or for what they may become, are its museums, its National Art Gallery, its Royal Mint and the Archives Building, which houses a collection of extremely valuable historical documents.

IV

LANDS AND THE PEOPLE

IN my last chapter I mentioned the ungranted public lands as amongst the assets of the Dominion. Apart from the vast area of land north of the limits of the provinces, the Crown, according to a recently published official estimate, still holds the title to many millions of acres of "ungranted, surveyed public lands in Manitoba, Saskatchewan, and Alberta in addition to a vast quantity of good land yet unsurveyed." The public lands in the Eastern Provinces are owned by the provinces, but in every section of Canada lands may be obtained by the *bonâ fide* settler, either as free grants, or at a very small rate of payment. This matter will, however, be referred to again later.

Lands offered for settlement in the provinces of the middle west are laid out in blocks six miles square, called townships. Each of these townships is divided into thirty-six sections of one mile square. The sections are again divided into quarters; and the homesteads offered as free grants by the Dominion government on certain conditions as to residence upon and improvement of the land; each contain one-quarter section, or one hundred and sixty acres. (For the land regulations as to free grants and pre-emptions, see Appendix, Note B, p. 160.) Within a certain area two sections in each township have been allotted to the Hudson's Bay Company, two are reserved for the support of schools, sixteen are held for sale or have been given as land grants in aid of colonization railways, and the remaining sixteen are, or have been, open to homesteaders.

During the fiscal year of 1911-12, over thirty-nine thousand heads of families, or single men, made homestead entries, taking up over six and a quarter millions of acres. In the same year the railway companies and the Hudson's Bay Company sold between eighteen and nineteen million acres of land; and it is predicted that before another decade has gone by "Canada's balance of population will be west of Lake Superior." This may or may not be true, for there is no province in Canada that is not well able to support a much larger population than it has at present; and in every province new opportunities are offering themselves.

In connection with its ownership of the crown lands, the Dominion government assumed at Confederation the guardianship of the Indians, descendants of the ancient lords of the soil. In the drama of Canadian history, especially in its earlier scenes, the Indians play a part that is tragically interesting, whether regarded from the point of view of the settlers, or from that of the wild people themselves, as they were driven deeper into the wilderness, and sank gradually from the position of being reckoned with and feared into that of a comparatively feeble folk, bewildered by the necessity of adaptation to new conditions.

The Canadian Indians, though of many different tribes, have been placed by ethnologists in three or four chief groups. The largest group numerically, and the most widespread, was the Algonquin, to which belong the Micmacs of Nova Scotia, the Ottawas and Ojibways of Central Canada, the Crees of the Middle West, and many other tribes.

A second group—the Huron-Iroquois—was, in many respects, remarkable. The Iroquois tribes are notable for having entered into a confederation from which they were often called "The Five Nation Indians." This alliance gave them a vast advantage over isolated tribes in their savage warfare; and made them for the best part of a century a menace and a terror to the French. They occupied a very advantageous position in what is now New York State, upon a "Height of Land" from which flowed streams in every direction, serving as waterways for their canoes and enabling them to descend with ease and rapidity into the enemy's country. They were usually friendly to the English colonists; but again and again during the early days did their utmost to destroy the infant settlements of the French and to annihilate the latter's Indian allies.

Many years later the famous Mohawk, Brant, and others of the Iroquois sided with the English in the Revolutionary War, and at its close were granted lands like other loyalists in Canada. The city of Brantford, on the Grand River, was named after the chief, and near to it is the "Mohawk Reserve," comprising over forty-three thousand six hundred acres, where some four thousand Indians still dwell.

Akin in race and language to the Iroquois, but in a constant state of hostility to them, were the Hurons, living near the Georgian bay. Amongst them, in the seventeenth century, the Jesuit fathers from France established, at great sacrifice of ease and comfort, a flourishing mission, but in 1648-49 the mission villages were swept out of existence by hordes of Iroquois; many of the missionaries were martyred, and the Hurons, utterly broken, were driven to seek refuge near the French towns.

The Iroquois and Hurons were in some respects more advanced than the Algonquin tribes. They had the art of making strong palisades about their towns, of several concentric rows of tree trunks planted upright in the ground, and they used shields of skin and a curious armour of twigs interwoven with cords, which formed a great protection against arrows. They also cultivated the ground to some extent, grew maize and sunflowers, and kept hogs. The Algonquins, on the other hand, trusted for food entirely to hunting and fishing, and to what they could gather in the woods.

None of the Indians had a written language, but some practised picture-writing, that is, making rude drawings on bark or skins for the conveyance of information; and they used also to weave shell beads, called "wampum," into collars and belts of curious devices, which represented certain ideas. These belts were used as mementoes and records of matters of importance, such as a treaty made with another tribe; and were given into the custody of old men who were expected to remember and explain their signification.

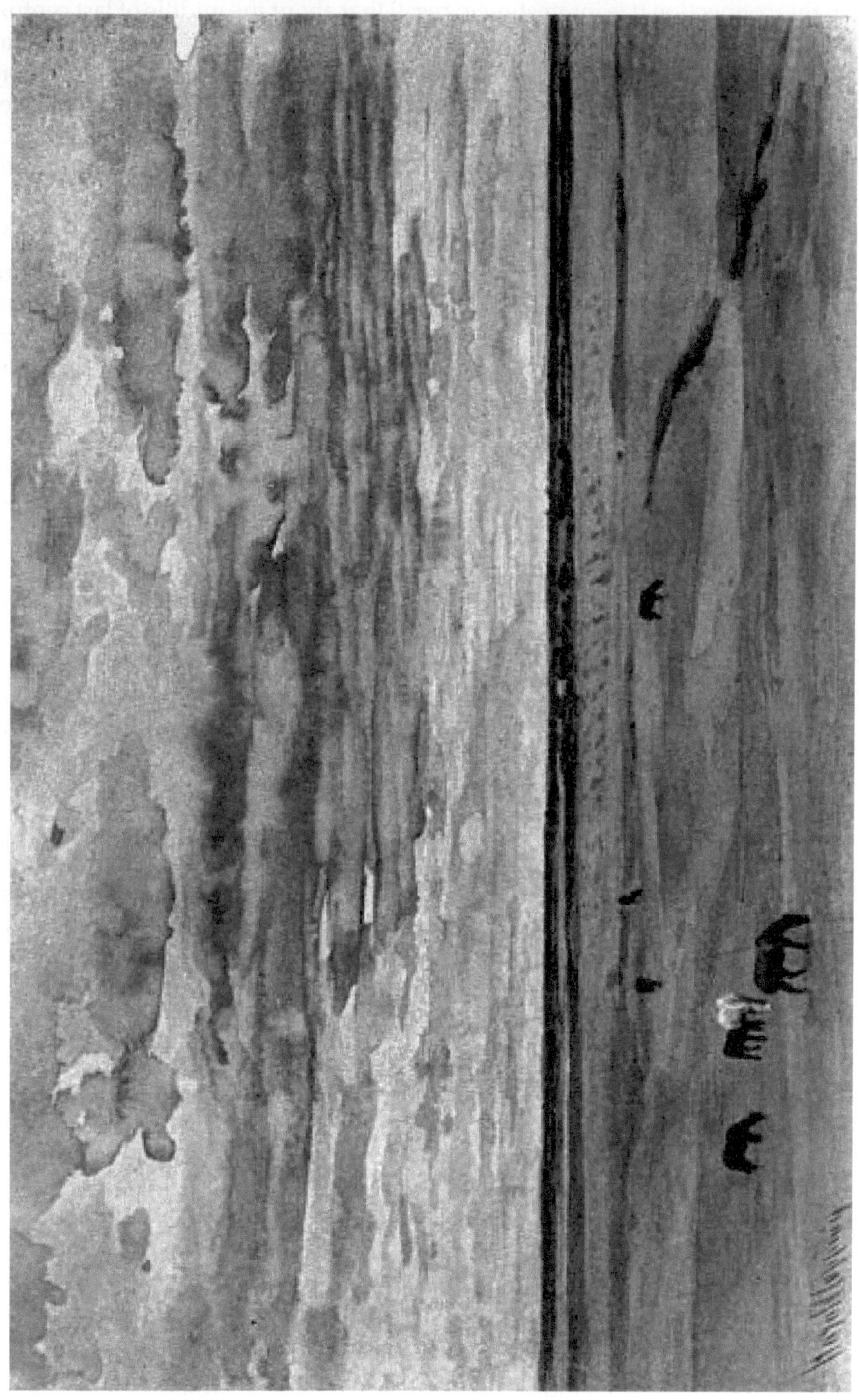

THE PRAIRIE AT ELSTOW, SASKATCHEWAN.

In this connection it is interesting to recall that about the middle of last century, a Methodist missionary, Evans, invented a method of writing the Indian languages, which can be learnt by an Indian of ordinary intelligence in a very few lessons. The signs represent syllables, not letters to be combined into syllables. This system of reducing the languages to writing has made possible a very large circulation of the Bible, or parts of it, amongst Indians, who would have had no opportunity of learning to read by such methods as our own. Liberal provision, however, has been made for the education of the Indians dwelling in the more settled regions.

A third great group of the aborigines of Canada comprises the Indians of the western mountains and the Pacific Coast and islands. These tribes were generally fierce and warlike; and were remarkable for their huge canoes, each made from the trunk of a single tree; for their enormous, grotesquely-carved totem poles; and for many singular customs.

Scattered along the thousands of miles of Canada's northern coasts are the Eskimos—"eaters of raw flesh"—or Innuits—"the People" as they call themselves. From a consideration of some of the resemblances in their implements and ornaments, made of bone and antlers and teeth of animals, and decorated with spirited drawings of men and beasts—some scientists believe them to be akin to "the Cavemen," of whom traces have been found in France and Great Britain. Their hovels (often half underground) of earth and turf resemble caves; but they have been known to turn bones to account for building material, and everyone knows of their habit of making a temporary shelter of snow built up in blocks into a curious beehive-like shape. They are a stout, sturdy people, who, living under conditions which the white races find almost unendurable, are remarkable for cheerfulness and good humour.

In 1871, when the first Dominion census was taken, it was estimated that the Eskimo and Indian population numbered a little over 102,000. In 1912, the number of Indians was returned at 104,956, an increase of nearly 1,300 since the census taken in the previous year. In some districts the Indian population is decreasing; in the older provinces, where the Indians are more civilized, there is an increase. That it is very difficult to form an exact estimate of the numbers of the wild people of the Dominion is shown by the very recent discovery of a hitherto unknown tribe of Eskimo, in the Coppermine River district, east of the mouth of the Mackenzie.

Upon the whole the early French settlers and rulers treated the Indians with more consideration and generosity than did the English colonists. In many instances, indeed, the French bushrangers and their leaders (though the latter were not infrequently of gentle birth and education) carried their complacency to the Indians so far as to adopt their manners and habits of life, sinking themselves almost to a state of savagery. The better aspect of the situation, however, appealed to the men who conquered Canada, and the British government of the country has, in the main, like its predecessor, treated the Indian with consideration and justice.

As the land has been required for white settlement, the government has entered "into treaty" with its Indian possessors, setting apart reserves for them and making allowances of money for their support and education. The Indians of the

Dominions are in very different stages of civilization; in fact, a small minority are still pagans, practising polygamy, and various heathen rites. There are in different parts 325 Indian schools, having on their rolls the names of 11,300 pupils. A few of the more progressive Indians have taken advantage of provisions in the law by which they may obtain the electoral franchise; but many are still content to remain "the Wards of the Nation," a position which some people think not wholly desirable for adults of any race.

From the consideration of the ancient people of the land, it is a natural transition to the newcomers. In the history of the Dominion there has been a recurrent high and low tide in the coming of settlers. But its flood has never before reached such proportions as within the last decade; and the most recent year for which the figures are attainable shows an immensely larger number of new arrivals than ever before. Of the total number of immigrants in the sixteen years ending March 31, 1912, nearly three-quarters were English-speaking people from the British Isles and the United States; but the remaining quarter represents an amazing number of nations, peoples and languages, the absorption of whom is one of the most difficult problems which Canada has to face. In the year of 1911-12, 82,406 foreigners came into the country.

In every large city it is coming to pass that there is a markedly foreign quarter; and many of the older people remain foreigners to all intents and purposes. The women especially, mixing less with their neighbours than the men, are usually slow to learn English; but the children pick it up quickly, and with it some at least of the ideas (good and bad) of the new land. Some of the foreigners come to Canada with the hope of making money and returning to their native countries; but many are anxious to remain. An alien, before making entry for a free grant of land, must declare his intention of becoming a British subject; and is obliged to be naturalized before he can receive a legal patent to the land upon which he has done homestead duties. But he must live three years in Canada before he can be naturalized.

The American immigrants are usually of a class which the Dominion particularly needs, many of them being farmers, who have had experience under somewhat similar agricultural and climatic conditions in the north-western States. They frequently bring not only experience, but a considerable amount of capital and stock; and altogether, being in a position to make the best of the country, they win success for themselves and demonstrate the capabilities of the land, in a fashion which the man from the "Old Country," especially if he be town-bred, can rarely at once attain. Their methods have the advantage also of giving an object-lesson to other less experienced immigrants, which save the intelligent and those willing to learn from making blunders.

As to the political view of the matter, the coming of these farmers from across "the line" does not as a rule give much anxiety to Canadians with regard to its effect on the permanence of the British connection, for the newcomers generally are satisfied that they have as much liberty under the Canadian system of government as under the American; and the most restless of them are more keenly occupied with money-making than with politics. Sometimes, however, the galling of the protective tariff, which presses unequally on different classes, provokes loud protests from the agricultural populations, particularly in the West; and there are signs that these protests will grow more vigorous and insistent with time.

The city-bred British immigrant is distinctly at a disadvantage with regard to experience, but if he is willing to take measures to learn before embarking in farming or any other enterprise with the details of which he is unfamiliar there is no reason why he, too, should not succeed. If the British immigrant has the appearance of being likely to "make good," no one is more gladly welcomed than he; but no immigrant of any nationality unlikely to succeed gets a welcome at all.

The question, "Are Canadians loyal?" with reference to such matters is sometimes much discussed. From long experience in the country, I should answer the question broadly in the affirmative. I should be even inclined to think that the Canadians value the British connection more highly to-day than twenty or thirty years ago; and that the strength of sentiment towards the British sovereign and "the Empire" has increased with the increase of the liberty granted by the Mother-land to the Dominion to work in her own way towards her ideal of nationhood. Whatever may have been the case in the past, at present I firmly believe that that ideal is one of a free nation within an Empire, bound together by those ties of kinship and similarity of ideal and sentiment (let us not blush to use the word) without which the coarser ties of common governmental institutions and commercial enactments become very brittle and often vexatious.

As a nation, Great Britain has long ceased the attempt, which ended so disastrously with her older American colonies, to exploit her "possessions" in the interests of her merchants and shipowners, and, of late years, she has adopted a very sympathetic attitude towards the natural desire of the free-born British peoples in the "overseas dominions" to be permitted to come of age nationally, and to have at least some control over their connections with the outside world. That this desire for control of their own affairs should involve responsibility for their own defence, Canadians are beginning to realize; but what direction the acceptance of this responsibility will take is yet undecided.

But to return to the immigrant. Strenuous efforts are made to bar the Dominion's doors against undesirables, including the physically and mentally unfit, and those so poor as to be in danger of becoming a burden on the community. Some people feel that the immigration regulations are too stringent, and are sometimes applied to individuals in an over-drastic fashion. It may be that in the anxiety to avoid possible burdens, the doors are sometimes shut against those who, given a chance, would prove a source of benefit to the new land, whose vast, empty acres cry aloud for people.

But whether or not the existing regulations could be improved upon, while they are in force, no wise man intending to settle in Canada will neglect to find out before starting what they are, and whether he can satisfy the requirements.

Many Canadians view the rapid influx of immigrants with anxiety, lest the Dominion should fail to assimilate these streams of new arrivals pouring in annually; and in a measure the severe restrictions on immigration are due to this anxiety. It is true in every land that the mistakes or successes of one generation may profoundly affect the well-being of generations to come; but in a country like Canada the public-spirited feel that blunders of to-day, possibly only affecting a mere handful of people, may be bringing misery on populations multiplied a thousandfold to-morrow. Happily it is not only blunders that are subjected to the process of multiplication and magnification; and in quietness and patience (scarcely noticed amidst the buzz of advertising and boasting of the great things to be) some people are earnestly labouring to begin the building of the new nation well; and perhaps are actually building better than they know. In the social freedom of the new lands, men and women of strong character count for much in either good or evil.

Upon the whole, the people of the Dominion are law-abiding. Unlike the republic to the south, the punishment of criminals has been made a matter of Dominion (instead of provincial) concern. The criminal law is one for the whole country, and justice is administered with a steady hand. In the prairie provinces, the North-West Mounted Police force, organized in 1873, has proved its efficiency in maintaining law and order through leagues of wilderness, in the lumber camps, and in the mines which draw together the roving and adventurous from every part of the globe. In 1913 the force consisted of some 50 officers and 576 men, distributed in 73 detachments in Alberta, 83 in Saskatchewan, 8 in the Yukon and several in the North-West Territories.

Compared to many European nations, Canadians are a temperate people, and in many municipalities there is "prohibition." Setting the present situation with regard to drunkenness against the state of things sixty or seventy years ago, the comparison is immensely in favour of the present day; for, in that early time, whiskey was manufactured in rude distilleries all over the country, and could be bought by the gallon for a few cents. Strong drink was expected by men working in the harvest fields or coming together in a threshing or raising "bee"; and many were the tragedies which resulted from this pernicious custom. Gentlemen counted drunkenness no disgrace, and it was a common fault of the officers of the garrison at Halifax and elsewhere.

In comparison, however, with conditions a few years ago, the showing is not satisfactory. In fact, it has been stated recently that "Canada's drinking and criminal record is increasing faster than the population." Some observers think that this is owing in part at least to the number of newcomers from less temperate countries, and "to the concentration of population in the large cities of the Dominion," but, at the same time, "progress towards the general adoption of prohibition is certain and rapid."

Taking Canada as a whole, excellent provision is made for education. The systems vary a little in the different provinces, but the common schools are everywhere free; and there are comparatively few native-born Canadians who cannot at least read and write.

THE BIG TREE, STANLEY PARK, VANCOUVER.

In 1910-11 Canada had over 1,197,000 pupils in her schools, and a small army of thirty-four thousand teachers, a very large proportion of whom are women. The schools are the chief of all the forces for the Canadianizing, if not of this generation of adult foreign immigrants, at least of their children. The central government spends hundreds of thousands of dollars annually on the education of the Indians, and in each province a very considerable proportion of all money devoted to public uses is spent for education. In the prairie provinces millions of acres of land have been reserved by the Dominion government to be sold gradually for the support of schools. All schools below the grade of High Schools are free to children between the ages of five and fifteen; and High Schools in all the cities and large towns are free to resident pupils. The number of children for whom a school district can be organized in the western provinces varies from eight in Alberta to twenty in British Columbia.

With the exception of Prince Edward Island, which can take advantage of the universities in neighbouring provinces; and of British Columbia, which has colleges at Vancouver and Victoria affiliated with McGill University, and has recently set apart two million acres of public land for the endowment of a provincial university—each province has one or more universities. The University of McGill at Montreal is the richest of Canada's universities; and that of Toronto, with over 4,100 students in 1913, is the largest.

An interesting fact in connection with all Canadian universities is that a large proportion of their students are drawn from classes by no means wealthy; and numbers of the undergraduates are "putting themselves through," as it is sometimes called. Many of these, having been engaged as teachers or in some business, have saved a sum of money for the payment of the expenses of part of their course. To eke this out, they seek employment in the long summer vacation, which, happily for them, coincides with the busy season, when men are in demand for every form of work; and a resolute student usually finds something to do. If he is not of the physique to go into the harvest fields, he may find employment as a timekeeper over a gang of foreign labourers, a waiter in a summer hotel, or a teacher in some scattered settlement which can only aspire as yet to a summer school. Given reasonably good health, a determined man will usually find or make a way to earn something in the summer; and such are the men who make the most of what can be gained from their hard-won courses of instruction in the winter.

At intervals people lift up their voices in protest over the readiness with which poor men's sons can rise into the professional classes, and imagine that it accounts, in part at least, for the continuous movement townward from the country districts; but there would surely be more loss than gain to Canadian life in general if any class of young people could be shut up by lack of wealth or other disability to the vocation of their fathers. Canada, though it has a growing wealthy class, and, alas, a growing submerged one, is a long way yet from the fixed "caste" idea.

The healthier recognition of a possible connection between the aspiration for college education amongst country-bred youths and the deserted farms in some of the older provinces, is the attempt made to lift agriculture to its true position amongst the great industries as a scientific profession. For long years agricultural societies have been working to stimulate the ambition of farmers in their own line of work. But this was not enough. It is possible for a dullard and an ignoramus to pick a meagre living from amongst the weeds of a neglected farm; but it takes not only brains, but cultivated brains, to farm well. No man is too good, whatever a "smart" lad may think, for the foundation industry of the world; and no farmer can have a too good educational equipment for this work. Perhaps the people of the Dominion, when reviewing what has been done in this country for education, have a reasonably good right to look with pleasure on the effort to bring well-trained minds to bear on agriculture. At sixteen different points in the Dominion, there are Government experimental farms, and the result of their work in testing seeds and methods suitable to various soils and conditions, finding out good stock and so forth, are at the free service of the farmers. Nor is this all. For nearly forty years Ontario has had in the Agricultural College at Guelph, a school, at once practical and scientific, for farmers; and this is only one of several agricultural colleges, while in the new University of Saskatchewan, one of the first departments to be organized was that of agriculture.

In connection with the colleges and universities are short courses—in England they would probably be called "University Extension" lectures—on agriculture and subjects related to the farm, especially designed for the benefit of dairymen, threshermen, housewives, beekeepers, etc., etc. The imparting of the special knowledge to make a scientific instead of a blundering amateur "thresherman" fits in oddly at first sight with one's preconceived notions of a university; but why should the extension downward in such utilitarian directions—the striking deep of its roots into the common earth—prevent a great educational institution flowering freely in the higher realms of science and art and philosophy?

There is another aspect to the case. I was much interested, a few months ago, on a chance conversation in a train with an old western farmer of rugged aspect, by his remark that the institution of college and university courses in agriculture would tend to raise the young fellows of the farming classes in their own eyes and in those of other people, and would also enable them better to hold their proper place in the country. (I give the substance of his remarks, not his words.) Now, it is a fact that the Canadian farmer is, as a rule, a much less self-assertive and a more retiring being than his brother—the doctor, the merchant, the manufacturer, the lawyer or the politician, as the case may be; and sometimes his interests suffer on account of his modesty. Nevertheless, there are not a few men amongst the farmers who are of excellent intellectual capabilities. They are men who think, moreover, and some day, now that they are beginning to organize themselves, the result of their thinking will have considerably more effect on the public life of the Dominion than it has had hitherto.

In the various provinces there has been a widespread movement of late years in the direction of the formation of farmers and country-women's clubs or institutes, which not only serve as a means for the dissemination of information, but give a much-needed stimulus to the social life of thinly settled districts, where hitherto (in the case of the women especially) the churches have been the chief social factor.

The churches will continue, both in town and country, to be of account in the social side of life, apart from their primary importance as definite religious agencies. According to the latest census there were in Canada over 2,833,000 adherents of the Roman Catholic church, which gains immense strength from its solidarity. The Protestants, on the other hand, though stronger numerically, are split up into numerous divisions, and in hundreds of little villages throughout the Dominion, there are three or four churches of different denominations, whilst numberless other places have no church at all. This over-lapping adds immensely to the toils, and perhaps detracts from the efficiency, of the country ministers and missionaries as a body. But projects of union are in the air, and there is hope that the several great Protestant churches may devise some plan of working together much more than has been done hitherto, even if they do not accomplish the corporate union which many of their adherents desire. In numerical strength the Protestant churches come in the following order:—Presbyterians, Methodists, Anglicans, Baptists, and a large number of smaller organizations. Apart from definite efforts by the churches themselves to arrive at some basis of union, there are numerous inter-denominational associations which are tending towards unity. One of the most notable of these is the organized effort, known as the "Laymen's Missionary Movement," to arouse the interest of business men in missions. This organization, first started in the United States, has resulted in largely increased giving for missionary purposes.

The immense immigration to Canada of foreigners and others necessitates constantly increasing effort on the part of the churches to keep abreast of their duties and opportunities; and amongst the numbers of newcomers there is much call to foreign missionary work within the borders of the Dominion, if it is to remain, in anything more than name, a Christian country. For instance, Montreal and Toronto each have thousands of Jewish citizens, many of them from Russia and other foreign lands. Galicians, adherents of the Greek Church, are numerous in the prairie provinces; and there are over fifteen thousand Mormons in Canada, chiefly in Alberta and Ontario. As farmers they are said to be excellent settlers; whether or not they will be equally successful in sowing the seeds of their distinctive tenets, so degrading to women and to the sanctity of home life, yet remains to be seen. It is, however, only fair to add that the Mormons in Canada do not, as in Utah, practise polygamy openly.

In British Columbia, and to a less extent throughout Canada, are to be found numbers of quiet, industrious Chinamen, working on the railways, in the hotels of the West, in the canning factories of the Pacific Coast, and in laundries from Victoria to Halifax. Despite the heavy head tax of $500 (£100) on each newcomer, no less than 6,083 Chinamen came to Canada in a recent year. Amongst them are very few women; but a number of young boys have recently been brought out by their relatives to attend the public schools, with a view to their learning English and the "Western learning" that goes with it.

The records of the British and Foreign Bible Society are suggestive in connection with the influx of foreigners into the Dominion. In 1912 sales were made of the Bible, or portions of it, in 44 languages in Toronto alone; and of 110 languages in all Canada. The earliest foreign version of the Scriptures issued by the Bible Society in its first year—1804—was, by the way, that intended for the Mohawk Indians in Canada. Many organizations, such as the Women's Christian Temperance Union, the Young Men's and Young Women's Christian Associations and the Salvation Army are doing their useful work all over Canada. There is indeed great scope for such organizations, for the Dominion is full of young people and friendless strangers, who in their loneliness are in great need of a helping hand.

But constantly fresh districts open beyond the reach of the churches and philanthropic agencies, and here the need is for individuals whose Christianity is deep enough to stand the hard test of isolation. Many immigrants (so-called Christian), when deprived of church services and the influences of old days, seem to forget their faith. But to those who hold fast their religion under the new trials may come the reward of giving an uplift to, and stamping a Christian character upon, a whole community. Indeed, a neighbourhood often reflects for years the type of its earlier settlers.

V

INDUSTRIES AND TRANSPORT

THE most important industry of Canada is, of course, agriculture, which employs nearly twice as many people as any other class of industries, and has a greater annual product. With comparatively few exceptions, the farmers of Canada own their own land. Considered from the point of view of its returns, the greatest crop is wheat. Saskatchewan ranks first as a wheat-growing province; Manitoba and Alberta coming respectively second and third. In the older provinces the farmers are going in to a great extent for mixed farming, and for the raising of apples and other fruit. British Columbia is also giving much attention to the fruit industry. At present many of the prairie farms are devoted solely to the growing of grain; but already the leaders of the agricultural world of the Dominion are urging the extension of "mixed farming," for the sake of saving the fertile soil from exhaustion and for the simplification of the labour problem, which is aggravated by the crowding of all the work of the farms into a few brief weeks of summer.

The second great industry of those depending directly on natural resources is lumbering. When the French settled on the St. Lawrence, they perceived at once the value of the forest wealth of the land, reporting to the home government that the colony would prove a rich source for the supply of masts and spars for the royal navy; and soon "stringent regulations were issued for the preservation of the standing oak." The early British governors were also instructed to take measures for the preservation of lumber likely to be useful for the navy.

The export of Canada's forest products began, it is said, in 1667, when the first shipload of lumber was sent to Europe. For years forest products came first in value on the list of exports. During the earlier part of the nineteenth century, Canada's lumber went chiefly to Great Britain; but during the last forty years much has been exported to the United States. This has, however, been offset in part by considerable imports of American lumber into Canada.

In Canada there is, of course, an immense domestic demand for wood. Over half the people live in wooden houses, immense quantities of wood are still used as fuel, our thousands of miles of railway tracks are laid on wooden ties or "sleepers;" fleets of wooden ships and boats still ply on our coast and inland waters—in fact, it has been said that "our civilization is built on wood. From the cradle to the coffin in some shape or other it surrounds us as a convenience or necessity." Our childhood's toys, our furniture, the very paper on which the news of the day is printed, are forest products strangely transmuted. No sane person would dispute the value of the forests, and Canada is richly endowed in this respect; though, perhaps, hardly so richly as some estimates would lead us to believe.

1. TRANSPORTATION IN THE WEST: CONSTRUCTION TRAIN ON THE GRAND TRUNK PACIFIC RAILWAY.

2. CANADIAN PACIFIC RAILWAY IRRIGATION DAM AT BASSANO, ALBERTA.

In time past there has been most reckless waste of the Dominion's forest wealth. In early pioneering days, perhaps it was unavoidable that the immigrants, far from markets, and hemmed in by great woods, should treat the trees as natural enemies, and clear them off the face of the earth as rapidly and as thoroughly as they could. So, in Ontario, were destroyed millions of magnificent trees; in many instances of kinds that would now be of immense value for the making of the better kinds of furniture; but black walnut trees were used to make fences of, and beeches and maples, too heavy to raft down the lakes to the seaports, as was done with the pine, were drawn together and burned in great heaps so that the settler could plant his first little crops of corn and vegetables amongst their stumps, and could turn an honest penny by selling the potash he made from their ashes.

Not only the pioneers, however, have been responsible for the destruction of trees. The Indians and hunters of game in the woods, the lumbermen, leaving their great heaps of dry brush and other inflammable refuse, only needing a chance spark from the lighting of a pipe, or a camp fire carelessly left burning, to turn it into kindling, ready laid for a great conflagration; the railways with the unguarded smoke stacks of their engines, have all had their share in the destruction of the forests; and it has been estimated that more timber has been destroyed in the Dominion by fire than by the axe. The nation is, however, awakening to the seriousness of the situation. For the last fourteen years the Canadian Forestry Association, with branches all over the Dominion, has been doing excellent work in disseminating information and rousing public interest concerning the preservation of the forests, and a new governmental policy has been inaugurated. Large areas of land have been set apart in Ontario and other provinces and by the Dominion government, where it has direct control, as "Forest Reserves."

In 1909 there was established the non-partizan "Conservation Commission," upon which each province is represented in the person of the cabinet minister most definitely connected with the administration of natural resources. Ontario's representative, for instance, is the Minister of Lands and Mines. The several universities of Canada are also represented. The functions of the Commission are advisory and educational, and its members are carefully studying the various natural resources. But it is recognized that the people are the greatest asset the country possesses; and while the Commission endeavours to devise plans for avoiding wasteful methods in lumbering and mining, to prevent the depletion of the fish in the waters and the game in the woods, it is concerned above all to discover means of stopping the fearful waste of human life by industrial accidents, unhealthy conditions, preventable diseases, and the ignorant treatment of infants and young children, which last results in such appalling mortality in the first five years of life.

It must not, however, be inferred from this reference to infant mortality that the climate of Canada is by any means unhealthy. The experience of immigrants from the British Isles and from all European countries shows that it is well fitted for Europeans; and, as a general rule, the children especially enjoy the cold months, finding delight in the sports that winter brings. Often the snow is too firm and powdery for that favourite sport of British youngsters—snowballing! But little ones who have not long learned to toddle alone can find amusement with their small sleighs, and for bigger children and young boys and girls there are the endless delights of "coasting" and tobogganning and skating and snow-shoeing and ski-ing.

Of course, here the country children have the best of it. But if one wants to realize the delights offered by a brisk winter's day, he cannot do better than visit some open hilly spot within the limits of one of Canada's cities—especially on a Saturday afternoon when the fathers have time to join in the fun. Then the white hillside is fairly alive with children in gay blanket-coats (often of scarlet) and knitted French-Canadian "tuques" ending in saucy bobs on the top, or long bag-like arrangements finished with dangling tassels; but it is the eagerness of the children and their quaint attitudes which give the picture its chief interest. A favourite way of making the descent is prone on the little sleighs, head foremost, legs stuck stiffly up from the knees, or trailing out behind, as an excellent rudder. Sometimes two "bob-sleighs," connected by a long board, form a more ambitious vehicle for half a dozen boys and girls at once, and loud are the shrieks and the laughter, as the "bobs" jolt over some rough bit of the track or shoot their passengers off at last into some heap of snow. As a rule, the mothers see that the youngsters are warmly clad in woollen garments from head to heel, and then no one is hurt by a roll in the soft snow.

But all this is, I am afraid, a long digression from the serious subject of industries. Canada's mineral products come next after those of the forest, and make a various list. It includes gold and silver, copper, nickel and lead; coal and iron; petroleum, natural gas, cement, clay products and building stones. These are widely distributed, and every day fresh discoveries are being made of deposits of useful minerals. In several instances the cutting of railways has led accidentally to such discoveries. This was the case with the copper ores at Sudbury and the silver at Cobalt; but scientists sent out by government and prospectors are always busily searching for new mineral fields. The central provinces of Canada import immense quantities of coal; though both in Nova Scotia to the east, and Alberta and British Columbia to the west, there are immense coal beds, which are being worked at the present time.

Government has made great efforts by the giving of bounties and by protective legislation to stimulate the manufacture of iron in this country. The result is that Canada, which in 1883 had only three or four small blast furnaces, had in 1913 eighteen furnaces, many of them large and of an up-to-date type, employing 1,778 men.

The fisheries of Canada are one of her greatest assets. In fact, it has been claimed that they are the most extensive in the world. But here, as with lumber, untold recklessness has reigned for generations, with the result that in some of the great lakes the fisheries are of much less value than they used to be. It is so with Lake Ontario, in which case the Americans must share the responsibility of depletion with the Canadians. Accounts of the catches of salmon and white fish made in the lake in the pioneer days read now like fables.

But the coast waters of the Maritime Provinces and British Columbia, and hundreds of the lakes in the interior, still abound with fish, and for a number of years "conservation" of the fisheries has been receiving careful attention. There are close seasons in fishing, regulated by act of parliament, to prevent reckless destruction, and there are now forty-one fish-breeding hatcheries.

Government has endeavoured to stimulate the fishing industry by a system of bounties; by establishing intelligence bureaux, with reporting stations along the coasts of the Maritime Provinces, which give "timely warning to the fishermen of a strike in of fish, of the weather and of other facts, early information about which is important to success." Cold storage establishments at different places for the keeping of supplies of bait have also been helpful to the fishing industry.

In the year 1911-12 the value of the fish taken and of fish exported was greater than ever before, but the figures of the returns do not by any means represent the whole value, for fish is used extensively as food, wherever it is caught. In order of value, salmon, caught chiefly on the Pacific Coast, comes first on the list of Canadian food fishes, the worth of the catch last year amounting to $10,333,000 or about £2,067,000. Next in order come cod, lobsters (of which fifty millions were caught in the year), herring, halibut, and oysters. In addition to fish, 1,244 whales were taken in Canadian waters. Canada's inland sea—Hudson Bay—is said to be one of "the richest whaling grounds in the world." It is also believed to be richly supplied with valuable fish of many kinds, but its fisheries are yet inaccessible to markets and are undeveloped. The great northern lakes are full of valuable fresh-water fish. Nearly a hundred thousand men, including those who work on shore, find employment in the fisheries.

From the fisheries the next step is naturally to the shipping interests. 1912 was a year of great expansion in the industry, and Canada moved from the tenth to the ninth place in the list of shipping nations; but she was fifth in the year 1874, at which period many ships were built in her yards. The reason for the falling off was the change from wooden to iron and steel ships. But the shipbuilding industry is beginning to revive, and at seven different points on the Atlantic, the Pacific, the St. Lawrence, and the Great Lakes, there are large dry docks for the construction and repair of vessels. In this connection it may be of interest to remark that the first vessel to cross the Atlantic under steam the whole way was the "Royal William," built at Wolfe's Cove, near Quebec, in the winter of 1830-31. Her historic voyage was made in 1833 from Pictou, in Nova Scotia, to London.

If the tonnage of vessels owned in Canada shows a decrease from the figures of forty years ago, it is hardly necessary to say that this is by no means the case with the tonnage of vessels required for the transportation of freight and Canadian passengers. In fact, little over one-tenth of Canada's exports is carried in Canadian vessels. The shipping employed is divided (so far as statistics are concerned) into three branches, according to whether it is employed in the overseas carrying trade between Canada and other countries; the inland lakes and rivers transport service; and the coasting trade, which, oddly enough, includes the activities of vessels voyaging from a Canadian port on the Atlantic, round Cape Horn to another Canadian port on the Pacific. The opening of the Panama Canal will enable these "coasters" to shorten their journey from Montreal to Vancouver (for example) by

7,221 miles.

Perhaps no nation is more favoured than Canada in the possession of inland waterways—though to take advantage of them to the present extent (and great expansion is possible) has required the construction of numerous canals and locks, to overcome differences of level; and, in some instances, to connect natural systems of navigable water. There is one great inland waterway in Canada, from the mouth of the St. Lawrence to the head of Lake Superior, by which large steamers can make a voyage equal to that from the mouth of the St. Lawrence to Liverpool. In this distance of two thousand two hundred miles there are only seventy-three miles of canals, with forty-eight locks overcoming five hundred and fifty-one feet of height.

Already, it is stated, the tonnage passing through the Sault Ste. Marie canals to avoid the rapids between Lake Superior and Huron is in amount three times that which passes through the Suez canal. By this route immense quantities of grain are brought to the ocean ports; and it is anticipated that within a short time when the deeper Welland canal is completed, ocean-going steamers will be able to carry their cargoes, without transhipment, all the way from the Lake Superior ports to those of Great Britain.

What this will mean to the Canadian West is evident, when one considers the cheapness of water-carriage compared with railway transport. The advantage of the former is indeed so great that, when time is not a primary consideration, freight from Liverpool for Vancouver or Victoria is carried all the way round by Cape Horn in preference to sending it by the more direct route to St. John or Montreal, and thence by rail across the continent to its destination. The first attempt to improve artificially the inland navigation was made in 1779, when canals were begun to overcome the rapids immediately above the Lachine rapids. But there are miles upon miles of navigable lakes and rivers in the Dominion which have needed no improvement.

Nevertheless, though the importance of the inland waterways can hardly be over-estimated, it is perhaps not too much to say that the Dominion of Canada has been made by her railways, for it was these which made possible a real union between the widely separated provinces of her earlier years; and the American description of "the Canadian Pacific Railway" as the "Dominion on wheels" expressed a most interesting fact. The building of railways began in 1836—with a sixteen-mile line (on which horses instead of locomotives were first used) between Laprairie, near Montreal, and St. John's on the Richelieu. Three years later another short line of six miles was made in Nova Scotia, upon which a steam-engine was used to draw coal from the Albion mines to New Glasgow.

It was not till the fifties that railway building in Canada was begun in earnest; but before that decade had half gone by, there were five hundred and sixty-three miles of railway, and by 1867 this length was multiplied by four. Since Confederation Canada's miles of railway have been multiplied almost by twelve, exclusive of sidings. Piling up figures, however, is a tiresome way to tell what is really a very interesting chapter in the history of Canada.

The railways linking Canada together have, indeed, cost the people and the Dominion and the provincial governments millions of money; and in early days, many municipalities, for the sake of having railways, seriously embarrassed themselves with debt. But the need seemed great. Lord Durham advised the building of the "Intercolonial Railway"—the line owned and operated by the Dominion government—to knit together the Maritime Provinces with the Canadas; but the difficulties and delays over this railway were endless, and it was not completed till 1876. For many years it was operated at a loss, but it has developed the country through which it passes and has greatly increased the trade between the several eastern provinces.

Before the era of railways, dwellers in New Brunswick who wished to go to Quebec used not infrequently to go on foot through the intervening wilderness in the winter time. So the first Lieutenant-Governor of New Brunswick once tramped through the snowy woods to visit his brother the Governor-General, Lord Dorchester; and so in 1813, when the war with the United States was raging, some companies of New Brunswick troops marched on snowshoes to the aid of their hard-pressed brethren in Canada. Much later, if a traveller wished to go from Nova Scotia to Toronto, it was the easiest way to take ship to Boston, and go thence through the "States" by rail to "Canada"—as the Nova Scotians continued to call the provinces touching on the St. Lawrence for long after the name was extended to the whole Dominion. This journey to "Canada" was quite an adventure to an untravelled person who had been born and brought up almost within sound of the sea. But the long-delayed construction of the "Intercolonial" gradually changed that condition of affairs.

The Grand Trunk is the pioneer of the several great company-owned railway systems, having absorbed many of the smaller railways begun in the fifties. For years it was not a profitable undertaking to its shareholders; but now its lines make a regular network in the older portions of Canada; and the Grand Trunk Pacific is being rapidly pushed to completion north of its older competitor in the West, the Canadian Pacific Railway. It is expected that when this "National Transcontinental Line" is finished it will shorten the trip round the globe by a week.

It is helping, moreover, to give Canada breadth from south to north. Already settlers are going into the so-called "Great Clay Belt" of good agricultural land in Northern Ontario. Already a string of little towns has sprung up along the Grand Trunk Pacific in the western provinces. Already its new seaport—"Prince Rupert"—five hundred and fifty miles north-west of Vancouver, and five hundred miles nearer to the east than any other Pacific Coast port, is an accomplished fact, where a population of four or five thousand is impatiently awaiting the uniting of the two portions of the railway which are being built westward and eastward, to meet in the mountains. Prince Rupert is close to some of the best fishing grounds in the world; and when the Grand Trunk Pacific line is completed it will put the fisheries of the North Pacific Coast in touch with a host of new markets.

It is difficult for people who have lived always in small well-settled countries to imagine what the opening of a great new railway means to the Dominion.

Over seventy years ago the people who see visions and dream dreams were prophesying a new trade route between east and west, by which the teas and silks of China and Japan would be brought by steam power along rivers, canals and railways across what is now the Dominion of Canada. In 1846 Sir Richard Bonnycastle, lieutenant-colonel of the Royal Engineers, predicted "We shall yet place an iron belt from the Atlantic to the Pacific—a railway from Halifax to Nootka Sound—and thus reach China in a pleasant voyage." Three years later another officer of the Royal Engineers, Major Carmichael Smith, published a pamphlet urging the construction of an "Inter-oceanic railway from Halifax to the mouth of the Fraser river," with a map upon which he traced a line almost identical with the routes ultimately adopted for the Intercolonial and Canadian Pacific Railways. But it was not until 1870, when British Columbia agreed to come into Confederation on condition that the inter-oceanic railway should be built, that any definite step was taken towards the construction of Canada's first "transcontinental line."

In the following year surveys for the line were begun under Mr. (afterwards Sir) Sandford Fleming. But the end was not yet in sight. The construction of the line was an immense task to be undertaken by a country so young and so sparsely settled as Canada, and fourteen strenuous years of political strife and struggle against all kinds of difficulty were to pass before the last spike of the railway was driven by Lord Strathcona (then Sir Donald Smith) at Craigellachie in the Eagle pass.

To the company, which finally built the line, the government gave $25,000,000 (£5,130,000) in cash, an even greater value in portions of the road already constructed, and twenty-five million acres of land, scattered through the prairie provinces, and the Canadian Pacific Railway is now a very wealthy corporation, which carries on numerous enterprises outside the actual business of railway transportation. For instance, there is a fleet of seventy-three Canadian Pacific Railway steamships, most of which are large vessels sailing the Atlantic, the Pacific, and the Great Lakes. These ships carry annually over half a million passengers and give employment to over twelve thousand men. The company also owns a number of luxurious hotels, including the happily-named "Château Frontenac," which the new arrival from Europe, coming up the St. Lawrence, can scarcely fail to notice, crowning the rock of Quebec, near to the spot where old Count Frontenac, from his little "Château St. Louis," lorded it over the rough bushrangers and determined churchmen of New France.

The company still owns some ten or eleven million acres of land in the four western provinces; and during recent years has inaugurated a policy of irrigating some naturally rather arid lands in Alberta and preparing there what are known as "ready-made farms," for suitable immigrants. This experiment has inspired the governments of some of the provinces to make similar preparation for immigrant farmers. The preparation of the farms for their future owners is, of course, a business enterprize; none the less it has smoothed the way for many newcomers.

Looking at the map of the country served by the Canadian Pacific, we see no longer a line but a network of lines (even in the West) where fifty years ago it was generally supposed that nothing would grow. It is Canada's vast wheat fields, which have made possible her huge railway systems, and while new lands are year by year being brought under cultivation, the railways will continue to add to their mileage. On the other hand, every year the new lines of railway open fresh lands to settlers.

Another Canadian railway that has a remarkable record is the Canadian Northern, which claims to have grown at the rate of a mile a day for the last sixteen years. This railway also has obtained most liberal government assistance and is a transcontinental system in the making. In fact, contracts are let for the completion of the whole distance between the city of Quebec and Port Mann in British Columbia; but it has gone on the plan of building short lines in different districts, to be afterwards combined and connected to form the whole system. Already it has run many branch lines from Winnipeg—westward and northward and southward—into the great grain-growing districts, and in 1912 it hauled no less than sixty million bushels of wheat.

There are as well a number of smaller railways, and also a number of lines (1,308 miles in length in 1912) in which electricity is the motive power. Many of these are, of course, the street railways of cities and towns.

There is much of human interest connected with a great railway, dissipater of romance, destroyer of the picturesque, as it is generally asserted to be. Consider it from the large point of view of its inception, its planning, its organization; the political fight to gain for it a legalized existence and the support of public funds and grants of land. It may be that Canada has time and again been recklessly generous in the price she has given for her transportation schemes, and that she has paid too highly for the services of the forceful men able to overcome the difficulties of such enterprises—but railways and yet more railways is still her cry; and the Napoleon of finance who can organize the company to build them is counted worthy of a reward so rich that he and his associates may be tempted to grasp at more than their share of the good things that their line opens to the world, and to use their power not always for the public good. Canada needs the great organizers of industry and more of them; but she needs, too, statesmen ever watchful of the public interests, who shall know how to economize as well as how to spend, and shall be strong enough to keep control over, and use for the good of all the people, the different human forces which are engaged, blindly or wisely, selfishly or nobly, in making out of several comparatively weak provinces a big nation, which patriots hope and trust may be also a great nation.

From the other point of view, the subject of railways—as it touches the life and well-being of individuals in Canada—is also intensely interesting. Not long ago I talked with a man who had done well in the West, but had gone into a district ahead of the railway, expecting it to be made in a year. With this hope he had settled forty miles from his next neighbour, seventy-five miles from a post office, and fifty miles from the point where he had to market his grain; but instead of one year he had to wait ten for the promised line. No wonder that the dweller in the country places loves to see the train pass by. It means in illness, possibility of getting skilled help of doctor and nurse, in health, opportunity of intercourse with friends and neighbours; for the young and old, a fuller social life; for the farmer, access to markets and oftentimes prosperity instead of failure. In one word, it means opportunity in a thousand ways.

Of course, the railways employ a great army of men upon their construction on the one hand, and their operation on the other. In 1912 the C.P.R. alone had 85,000 employees on its pay rolls. The numbers finding employment in connection with the transportation systems in this "country of magnificent distances" as it has been called, would be vastly increased if those engaged in the subsidiary trades were taken into account, such as the making of iron rails, the construction of cars and engines, the cutting of railway ties and so forth.

A great change has taken place in Canada recently in the occupations of the people. Sixty years ago there were only twenty-eight or thirty different kinds of manufactures carried on in the country, and of the manufacturing establishments the chief were—shipyards, saw, grist, carding, and woollen mills; distilleries, tanneries, breweries and foundries, several of which are very closely connected with agriculture. The great woollen mills and the tanneries, for instance, are all closely dependent on farm products, as the saw mills are on the natural crop of wood, and all these with distilleries, in addition, were very early established on a small scale in the several districts to supply local demands.

By 1891 there were three hundred different kinds of manufactures, instead of thirty, and the number of workers employed had multiplied five-fold. Since then the capital invested, the value of their output, and the importance of Canada's manufacturing, has continued to increase, the development during the last decade being the greatest on record. Manufactures of wood and manufactures connected with food are still specially important.

Manufactures have been artificially encouraged by the so-called "National Policy," or tariff, arranged to protect home industries. One result of this has been the stimulation of the growth of the towns and cities. In Ontario the last census showed a considerable increase in the population as a whole, a greater increase in the urban population and a falling off of over 50,000 in the rural population. No doubt this is due in part to the exodus to the West, but the towns of Ontario can well support more than their old quota of population, and there are excellent markets near at hand for all the fruit, vegetables, and other farm products that can be raised. The same story comes from New Brunswick and that peaceful little agricultural community, Prince Edward Island.

The fact that Canada is becoming a manufacturing as well as an agricultural country is, however, in a large degree a natural development. There is no question that its opportunities are not confined to agriculture. It is, indeed, singularly favoured by nature with water powers, from which electricity for light and power can be developed readily and cheaply, and can be conveniently transmitted for hundreds of miles for use by great cities or by single farms.

As England's great coal fields determined that she should become a great manufacturing nation, Canada's immense number of cataracts and rapids promise that she, too, shall be great in the same line. Everyone has heard of the "harnessing of Niagara"; but not everyone realizes how much electricity is used in Canada. Many a little town, only a few months old, has stepped at once from the stage of lighting with lamps to that of brilliant electrical illumination. But if facilities for obtaining power are the first necessity for manufacturing, Canada has opportunities also in the variety of her natural products, from field, forest and mine. A third reason, strongest of all, perhaps, is that her people are ambitious, and rightly or wrongly feel that it is necessary to the realization of their nationhood that a proportion of their population should be engaged in manufacturing.

There is at least this strong excuse for such a position, that always there will be people to whom agricultural pursuits will not be congenial, and, if there were no opportunities apart from cultivation of the soil in Canada, many of her young people would continue to go elsewhere. At the present day, there are over a million Canadians in the United States, who have been attracted thither by the opportunities offered by its cities and industries. Some of these are now returning—drawn home to a great extent by the opening of new industries in their native land.

Unquestionably the prosperity of Canada rests mainly upon agriculture; and legislation that has any tendency to foster the growth of the towns at the expense of the country must in the long run prove injurious. Canada is, however, only following the example of older lands, when she rejoices in her big towns, and in the consequent massing of wealth in restricted areas, for the absence of these (at least as society is now constituted) limits the sphere of human activity; and, if Canada desires anything strongly, it is, perhaps, to be an all-round nation, possessing not only these material advantages of which we all hear so much, not only the chances for the honest worker, but also opportunities at least for the cultivation of science and art, literature and music. Now the cultivation of these is not easy in little frontier towns and hamlets and solitary farms deep in the country. But the manufacturing industries build up the towns, and the towns make possible a kind of co-operation in the things of the mind, that has been almost unheard of in the country.

Hasty visitors sometimes sweepingly and condescendingly accuse Canada of being "crude" and utilitarian, and of being in earnest chiefly about the pursuit of the "Almighty Dollar," and assert as a matter of course that the finer side of life is neglected, but often these critics would discover, if they stayed in the land a little longer, that much patient cultivation of the higher interests of humanity is going on beneath the surface, as it were. Moreover, if much and rich flowering has not occurred, the field—of human beings—is at present extremely small. The newcomer often expects at once much too much and too little, and makes his comparisons, forgetful of the fact that outstandingly great poets or painters, altruists and heroes are rare everywhere, and that they cannot be expected to be numerous in half a century of time, amongst a population of three or four or even seven millions. At Confederation, less than fifty years ago, Canada had only three and a quarter millions of people, and, for several decades after that, the growth was very slow.

Often, I would venture to say, that the "crudeness" complained of is as much in the surroundings as in the people themselves; and the critic from the Old World should not forget that, so far as the environment of the colonists is concerned, they often have nothing about them in the way of the refinements of life which they do not owe to themselves; whereas the beautiful city or house or church with which he contrasts their deficiencies of comfort or beauty was probably largely a heritage from past ages.

THE OLD SMELTER MINE, NELSON, BRITISH COLUMBIA.

But the reverse idea applies to the people themselves. Though they are dwellers in a new country, many overseas Britons are extraordinarily conscious of their own and their national past. They are more keenly conscious of what it stands for than many of the stay-at-home folk, who have some dim feeling that "colonists" (though their own sons and daughters) are people without a history and without a link to the great days and great deeds of their ancestors. His past is the cherished possession of many a Scot and many an Englishman, who has done brave work in building up the new country, and it seems rather like giving him "the cold shoulder" when a new arrival, flitting rapidly through the country, or even intending to cast in his lot with it, talks always of everything British as "ours," and of everything "colonial," as "*yours*." As Kipling suggests, the overseas Briton looks back to "the abbey" and much else that in the old land "makes us we," with no less love and veneration than the Englishman at home.

VI

THE OLD PROVINCE OF NOVA SCOTIA

I NOW propose to give some account of the nine provinces in succession, with regard to their extent, physical features, climate, natural resources, and the conditions and pursuits of the people. I shall also endeavour to give information as to the prospects in each province for immigrants from the British Isles. Of course, in the space at my disposal, I can touch but slightly on any of these points. I will begin with Nova Scotia, the province that lies nearest to England, though curiously enough it is little-known by English people compared to many of the more westerly regions. Except in winter, when the Canadian mail steamers cannot go to Quebec, and so land their mails and their cabin passengers at Halifax, Nova Scotia seems somewhat off the line of tourist and immigrant travel, which passes up the Gulf of St. Lawrence to the north of the little group of Canada's three "Maritime Provinces."

It is possible for anyone to live long in another part of Canada without getting much idea of the history, resources or characteristics of the "Provinces down by the Sea," but it adds immensely to one's interest and pride in the Dominion when one realizes that Quebec and Ontario—wealthy and important as they unquestionably are—are now only a part of Canada, and that for a comprehensive understanding of the country as a whole, there is needed at least some knowledge of the prairie provinces, and British Columbia to the west, and of the little old less restless Lower Provinces to the east.

The story of Nova Scotia is full of interest from the days early in the seventeenth century, when the first little company of French colonizers tried so gallantly to found Port Royal, down to the present time. The long struggle of the French and English for the possession of the land, the frightful deeds of their Indian allies, the coming of the Loyalists and other pioneers, the gallant fight for British liberty and "responsible government," all furnish incidents not less worthy of the poet's song than that pitiful deportation of the Acadians, which inspired Longfellow's pathetic but rather misleading poem of "Evangeline."

I can spare little space for history, but before I go on to tell what I can of Nova Scotia—and for seven years quaint old Halifax was my home—I should like to say that whatever else this smallest, save one, of the Dominion's nine provinces fails to produce, she has been singularly successful in the producing of men. Upon the roll of her "notables" are the names of Haliburton—"the father of American humour"—Inglis, who defended Lucknow; Cunard, founder of the line of great

Transatlantic steamships; Sir Provo Wallis, Admiral of the Fleet; Dawson, of geologic and educational fame; whilst other well-known names of men still at work might be added to the list.

The very name—Nova Scotia—forces comparison with old Scotland, but the former is not quite three-quarters the size of the latter, nor has it much more than one-tenth of the population. It is also far south of its namesake; in fact, there is almost eight degrees between the latitudes of the north of Nova Scotia and the south of Scotland, but the Arctic currents in the West Atlantic have their influence on the climate, making the Nova Scotian winter cold, and the spring late, though the extremes of heat and cold are not so severe as farther inland. During a recent year at Halifax, for instance, only once did the mercury fall to "zero," and only once in the hottest month, July, did it travel up to 98 degrees Fahrenheit.

On the Atlantic coasts there is a good deal of rain, fog and "Scotch mist," but summer and autumn are often delightful seasons of bright, clear, not too hot, weather. In the inland and western parts of the province the climate is drier and not quite so variable.

Like her namesake, Nova Scotia turns towards the ocean a deeply indented, forbidding coast; but the interior lacks "Old Scotia's" grand mountains, though it has a backbone of sterile hills running through the province, beside the Cobequid Mountains, in Cumberland County, and many a high rugged cliff in Cape Breton Island. This new Scotland has also its stretches of wild moorland and its lakes, set amongst dark spruce firs. But between "the barrens" of the Atlantic Coast, there is here and there a fertile valley; and on the Bay of Fundy side, but sheltered from its cold mists and winds by the long ridge of the North Mountain, stretches the far-famed Annapolis valley, where in spring the whole landscape seems one vast white orchard, save for the pretty little houses, half hidden amongst the bloom.

That side, too, is the region of the salt marshes, formed by the action of those phenomenally high tides of the Bay of Fundy, which were amongst the few remarkable features of Canada thought worthy of mention in the "Geographies" put into the hands of British children a generation ago. In course of ages these mighty tides have left vast level deposits of marine mud—the salt marshes—liable to invasion of the waves at spring tides, but easily turned by a little labour into pastures and hay meadows and grain fields of almost inexhaustible fertility. All that is necessary is to build dykes or embankments of tree trunks and clay to keep back the highest tides; and this work was begun long ago by some of the early French immigrants, who had been accustomed to reclaiming land from the sea in their own country. If, at any time, the fields should show signs of exhaustion, the fertilizing waters may again be let in for a short season; indeed, farmers living near undyked marshes are accustomed to haul loads of the precious sea-mud to their upland fields. Of something the same character as the dyked lands are the "intervales" along the rivers, which are said to be "invariably rich and productive."

FISH CURING AT GUYSBORO, NOVA SCOTIA.
NOTE THE SPLIT COD-FISH DRYING IN THE FOREGROUND.

The abundance of pasturage and hay makes good dairying, and Nova Scotia is emphatically a country of mixed farming. Almost all crops suited to a temperate climate can be grown in some part of the province. But, during a recent year, of all agricultural products, hay brought most money into the farmers' pockets; then came live stock products, potatoes, apples, oats, "garden truck," and so in a descending scale.

Not only the farming can be described as "mixed" in Nova Scotia. The occupations of her people (in number somewhat under half a million) are also mixed; and though agriculture takes first place, fishing, lumbering, mining and manufacturing are of importance, all the great industries setting "new records" last year.

In fishing, Nova Scotia was long the leading province of the Dominion, but in 1912, British Columbia, with her immense catch of salmon, stepped before her. In the Atlantic province, though the lobster fishery is valuable and is to the dwellers on the sterile southern coast the chief source of ready money, the cod fishery is worth most of all, a fact quaintly recognized by the habit of the shore people of referring to a cod as "a fish," and to all others of the finny tribe by their specific names of haddock, halibut and so forth.

The fishing hamlets consist of little whitewashed cottages dotted at random about the weather-beaten rocks, beside the fine natural harbours or little coves where the boats run in for shelter, alongside ramshackle stages where the cod are dried in the open air, and by fish-houses, often emitting the peculiarly horrible odour of over-kept "bait."

Despite all drawbacks, there is a fascination in the jumble of boats and nets and lobster traps, whilst the fisherfolk themselves, fresh-complexioned, clear-eyed, sturdy-limbed, simple, kindly and straightforward, are a good stock one would fancy to set against the threatening degeneration of the race by the unwholesome crowding into towns. Some 30,000 men find employment, on sea and shore, in connection with the fisheries. The fishermen are generally rather poor, but the more enterprizing members of the fraternity often pass from the sailing of a fishing boat to that of a coasting vessel.

In the coast villages tiny stores, with stock small in quantity, great in variety, are plentiful, and some of the fishermen attempt to add to their incomes by farming, often in a rather haphazard, amateurish fashion. Along the shore east of Halifax horses are scarce, and in the little hay-fields even a one-horse mowing machine is an unusual sight, and it is quite common to see two men, or it may be a man and a girl, carrying the cured hay to the barn on two stout poles. In those parts the fisherfolk take little pains even to improve their own fare by growing vegetables, but the soil is discouraging. In fact, one resident of a coast village near Halifax complained, "There ain't no soil. There's nothing but grits!"

Some of the fishermen prosecute their craft only "inshore," using small boats, remaining out but a few hours and fishing with hand lines as well as with trawls from the dories. These men are very dependent on the weather; but gasoline motor boats are coming into use, enabling them to go out when it would be impossible with sailing boats. The "bank fisheries," chiefly of cod, are carried on by schooners of about 100 tons, manned by twelve to twenty men, who go out, two by two, in dories, using trawls upon which are thousands of hooks. In the rivers, smelts, salmon, trout and eels are taken; and there are natural oyster beds, now yielding a few hundred barrels of oysters annually, which it is said, with improved management, may yield thousands. In fact, better methods may do much to make all the fisheries of Nova Scotia much more productive.

Of the forests of the province, something under one and a half million acres remain ungranted, and four or five times as much is owned by farmers and held or leased by lumber and pulp companies. As everywhere in the Dominion there has been untold loss from fires and wasteful methods, but the idea of "conservation" promises better things in future. Pine, of which there used to be large quantities, has become scarce; but spruce (of more recently discovered value) and birch, a good furniture wood, are extremely plentiful. The saw mills are generally situated on the rivers, near tide water; thus their product can be loaded directly into vessels, which carry it far and wide.

In several counties, a quantity of timber is used in the building of schooners and fishing boats, but the palmy days of shipbuilding in the province have passed. It may be, however, that there will be a revival, and that Nova Scotia will soon be sending forth iron (instead of wooden) ships to plough all seas, for she is richly endowed with mineral wealth. In fact, like Massachusetts, she seems to have every gift of nature—coal, iron, magnificent harbours, and not a little water power, all awaiting development—to make a great manufacturing region. Through her northern counties and Cape Breton Island stretches a rich and enormous coal field, and iron ores (scarcely touched as yet) are found in every county save one.

Nova Scotia ranks third of the provinces in manufactures, following the larger and much more populous provinces of Ontario and Quebec, but the value of her manufactured products (which include foods, textiles, chemicals, paper, vehicles, vessels and a variety of manufactures of iron and steel) has more than doubled in a single decade. Nova Scotia is said to have the "largest individual self-contained steel-making plant in the world," but the growth of the iron and steel industry is due not only to natural advantages and to the genius of different "captains of industry," but to the bounties and protective duties granted in its interests by successive governments of the Dominion.

Amongst the valuable minerals of the province are limestone, granite, gypsum and gold. The mining of the last-named metal has been carried on by rather primitive methods for nearly half a century. The yield for the record year was worth about $600,000 (£120,000), and at present three hundred men are employed at twenty-five different mines. There is one of these small mines in Guysborough County, on the edge of a vast stretch of "barrens"; but, despite its sounding name, "Goldenville" is a sorry little hamlet, of dingy, unpainted buildings, that seem to mock at the "prospector's dazzling dreams." But one does not usually go to an industrial place, large or small, in search of the picturesque. One may chance upon it there, however, as when at night the outpouring of molten slag from Sydney's black giants of blast furnaces suddenly lights up the wide beautiful harbour with a ruddy glow.

Halifax, the capital, containing nearly a tenth of the population of the province, is undeniably picturesque, with its old Citadel and churches, its wharves and its vessels, its odd outdoor market, its "redcoats" (now Canadians) and its coloured folk. Though on the eve of a great development of its port, which will doubtless revolutionize its business life, till very recently it has been a quiet old-fashioned place, its dinginess relieved by lovely water-views from many a point of vantage, and its dignity secured by such fine old stone buildings as the abode of the British admiral, Government House and the Province Building, where still, as in one other case, an Upper as well as a Lower House deliberates on the affairs of the province.

The Assembly of Nova Scotia, by the way, is the oldest representative body in the Dominion, having been convened for the first time in 1758. There was a long fight for the boon of responsible government, won in 1848; and the name of Joseph Howe, the Reform leader, son of a Loyalist, is renowned throughout the Dominion. During the last half-dozen years several imposing new buildings, including the Anglican cathedral and the Memorial Tower (commemorating the calling together of the first Assembly) have been erected in Halifax. The city is the terminus of the Intercolonial and two provincial railways, and has a variety of manufactures.

I cannot give space, as I should like, to descriptions of any of the smaller towns; but, though someone described Nova Scotia as "the province that was passed by," it is as truly a land of opportunity as any of the regions further west. The opportunity does not come in the shape of "free grants" of land, but a farmer who knows his business and has two or three hundred pounds of capital can soon own a good farm. There are farms of from fifty to three hundred acres of which the price is from $1,000 (£200) up. Some of these have been thrown on the market by the death or infirmity of their owners, some through the desire of a younger owner to go to the west or to take up work in a town. Amongst them are "run-down" farms, which can be obtained for little more than the cost of the buildings upon them, and a thoroughly capable farmer may sometimes find it pay to buy such a farm cheap and bring it back to good condition.

Within the broad realm of agriculture, to say nothing further of the other possible avenues to success in woods and mines and city and sea, there is variety of opportunity. Let a man decide to go into dairying, market-gardening, the raising of sheep, hogs or poultry, the culture of apples, or the growing of small fruits, and there is some part of Nova Scotia in which each one of these pursuits may be followed with special hope of success; moreover, the provincial government (which is frankly desirous of good immigrants of the right stamp) has made arrangements to help the new arrivals to find what they want. (For names of officials who will give information, see Appendix, Note A, page 159.)

With regard to the very profitable business of apple-growing, it is stated that not one-tenth of the land in the Annapolis valley and elsewhere suitable for orchards, has yet been planted.

As to the question of markets—the home market alone is an excellent one for practically all food supplies, for the constant influx of immigrants and the armies of non-producers engaged in mining and other industries create a demand in many lines of foodstuffs not easy for the farmer to overtake. Nova Scotia imports much that she might just as well grow. But aside from the home market, she has easy access to those of the other provinces, and to those of the United States and of Great Britain, for every one of her counties touches on the sea, which is the best possible highroad for freight. As to her internal means of communication, roads are improving and new railways are being added to the old.

With few exceptions, Nova Scotian farmers own the land they till, and to assist still more to do so, including newcomers, the provincial government makes arrangements with loan companies to lend as much as 80 per cent. of the appraised value of farm property on mortgage. The government is also authorized to buy "real estate in farming districts, subdivide this into suitable-sized farms or lots, erect buildings and fences thereon, prepare the land for crops and sell this improved real estate to newcomers on satisfactory terms." This opportunity to obtain ready-made farms will no doubt prove attractive to many newcomers.

In the fruit districts of Nova Scotia, owing to the smaller holdings, people are settled comparatively near together, and this is a great advantage so far as church and social life and the education of the children is concerned.

The elementary and high schools, supported by government grants and local rates, are free. In isolated communities it is sometimes difficult to obtain teachers; but a hopeful movement is the introduction of "consolidated schools," each of which, having several teachers, replaces the little "one-teacher schools" of a considerable district. There are now over twenty of these, to which the children are taken in vans.

Nova Scotia has several universities, supported by different religious bodies, in addition to the non-sectarian Dalhousie University at Halifax. The oldest of these institutions is King's College, at Windsor, which dates from 1790. A comparatively new institution is the Agricultural College at Truro. Here instruction is given free of cost to farmers, farmers' sons and new settlers intending to farm. Besides the full two years' course, there are short practical courses of two weeks, including one for women on dairying and poultry keeping. In connection with the college is a fine Model Farm, where excellent stock is kept. The government also maintains experts to give instruction in various branches of agriculture, and endeavours in a variety of other ways to improve the methods and conditions of farming in Nova Scotia.

There is a demand always for good farm workers and capable domestic servants. Even inexperienced young people have little difficulty in getting work, if they are strong and willing to learn, but they must not expect high wages till they are competent. For competent farm men the wages offered are usually from $20 (£4) to $30 (£6) the month, with board and lodging for a single man, and with a rent-free house and certain allowances of milk and vegetables for a married man. In the latter case, the wife, if willing to assist the farmer's wife, can often make a considerable addition to the family income. For day labour in the country a man might expect from $1 (4*s.*) to $1.50 (6*s.*), with board.

1. SIXTY ACRE ORCHARD, NOVA SCOTIA.

2. FARM HOUSE, NOVA SCOTIA.

In the towns wages are higher, even for unskilled labour, but in Halifax at least rents are very high, and a man who is looking forward to getting a little land of his own would usually be wiser to settle from the first in a country district where living is cheap, and where the experience gained would be of definite value in farming operations. Moreover, if he is able to keep a few fowls, and a pig, and have a garden of his own, it very much lessens the cost of living. There are many prosperous farmers in Nova Scotia who landed a few years ago with scarcely a shilling in their pockets, but these have been hard workers.

The population of Nova Scotia is chiefly of British descent, though not a few of the early settlers came by way of New England in Loyalist and pre-Loyalist days. Scottish names are common in many parts of the province, especially in Cape Breton Island. The ancient Acadians are represented by something like fifty thousand French people, and the Nova Scotians of German descent are not much fewer.

Of religious bodies, the Roman Catholics are the strongest, but the Presbyterians make a good second, then come in order the Baptists, the Anglicans and the Methodists. In the country places there are a few union churches, but there is a good deal of "over-lapping," which aggravates the difficulty of ministering adequately to communities so scattered, as they are, for instance, on the south coast.

VII

NEW BRUNSWICK, THE LAND OF THE ST. JOHN

THE Province of New Brunswick is in shape almost a square, and in extent has an area of about 28,000 square miles. In other words, it is smaller than Scotland, but has a much larger proportion of land that can be cultivated than that rugged little country which has sent forth such masterly farmers to till larger and richer fields than those of their own stern land. It is bounded on the east and south by the Gulf of St. Lawrence and the Bay of Fundy, which are separated by the narrow neck of land from which Nova Scotia thrusts itself like a great breakwater into the Atlantic surges. Northward it reaches to Chaleur bay and the Province of Quebec. Westward it is bounded by Maine, which (thanks to the efforts of a British diplomatist to settle at all costs a long-standing dispute) comes in like a wedge between New Brunswick and Quebec. In latitude New Brunswick lies almost entirely between the 45th and 48th parallels, which also, it may be noted, run across the central portion of France.

Upon the coast there is, as might be expected, a good deal of rain and mist and white sea fog; but the climate of the interior is more dry and clear; and there is no lack of sunshine. Compared with England, the winters are cold, and the farmer has a shorter period each year in which he can work upon his land; but in one of the government publications is given an interesting quotation bearing upon this point from a Report on New Brunswick, written in 1850, by a great English agricultural expert, Professor J. F. W. Johnston:—

> "On the whole," he says, "I think we must allow that though the period for out-door labour is shorter in New Brunswick—as it is in the Canadas, Maine, and the Northern States—than in England and in some parts of Scotland, yet that the action of winter upon the soil is such as to materially lessen the labour necessary to bring it into a proper state of tilth."

Moreover, while in Great Britain the work of the farmer is often interfered with by rain, and his expenses "considerably increased by the precarious nature of the climate in which he lives,"

> "In New Brunswick the climate is more steady and equable. Rains do not so constantly fall, and when they do descend, the soils in most parts of the province are so porous as readily to allow them to pass through. Thus the outdoor operations of the farmer are less impeded by rain, and the disposable time he possesses,

> compared with that of the British farmer, is not to be measured by the number of days at the disposal of each."

The climate of New Brunswick, the professor concludes,

> "does not prevent the soil from producing crops which, other things being equal, are not inferior in quantity or quality to those of average soils in England; while, as for its health, it is an exceedingly healthy climate. Every medical man I have met in the province, I believe without exception, and almost every other man I have conversed with, assures me of this, and the healthy looks and the numerous families of the natives of all classes confirm these assurances."

To this day the people of New Brunswick certainly have a healthy appearance, and rosy cheeks and clear complexions are common, especially on the coasts.

The winter of the interior is often described by the inhabitants, even in moments when they cannot be suspected of any thought of advertising the province, as a "good steady one." The fact is that most Canadians, either native-born or those who have lived long in the country dislike damp weather above any other kind. If the cold is only dry and clear, they do evidently from their behaviour feel it bracing, as they say; and it is the same with the summer heat, the days to be dreaded (if any?) are the days in which the atmosphere is humid as well as hot. The spring is late, and often almost before one realizes that winter is past one finds that summer is upon one.

New Brunswick is an amply-wooded land of pleasantly-diversified hill and valley, though its highest eminence, Sagamook or Bald Mountain, is only 2,604 feet above the sea. It is well watered by the Restigouche, the Miramichi and the St. John rivers, with their tributaries, and many smaller streams. The last-mentioned river is nearly five hundred miles in length from its sources in the wilds of Maine to its mouth. It is navigable for almost its whole length through the province, though in one place its course is broken by the "Grand Falls." Large-sized steamers go up as far as Fredericton, eighty-five miles from St. John; but there a change is made to smaller boats. The river flows for many miles through a fertile and beautiful valley; but as it approaches the city of St. John its banks become higher and bolder, and the stream widens out to a fine broad basin.

The gateway to the sea lies through a narrow gorge of less than five hundred feet, and here the current of the river makes fierce and constant struggle with the force of the famous tides of the Bay of Fundy. At St. John the normal rise is twenty-seven feet, and the result is the curious, but not quite happily-named phenomenon—the "Reversing Falls." At low tide the river tumbles and races in fierce haste down a sharp rugged slope to reach the bay; but the pressure of the incoming sea piles up the water of the harbour in the narrow channel to greater and greater heights, till, at the flood, the current of the St. John seems turned backward, and the tide water, as it comes plunging through the rock gateway, is at a distinctly higher level than the more peaceful surface of the river within. Happily at half-tide—four times in the twenty-four hours—there comes a brief truce in the everlasting struggle, and vessels can pass with safety to bear their freight of humankind and of all manner of merchandise up the grand natural highway of nature's making deep into the heart of the country.

ST. JOHN HARBOUR, NEW BRUNSWICK.

I do not propose here to dwell at any length on the history of New Brunswick; but I should like to say that, in common with every other province of the Dominion, it has a history—short in years, perhaps, but not devoid of human interest. If one were attempting to tell it, moreover, it would be impossible to do so without frequent references to the St. John. This river received its name three centuries ago because a little company of gallant French explorers, amongst whom was Samuel Champlain, afterwards founder of Quebec, discovered it upon St. John the Baptist's day.

In those old days, the broad bosom of the river was often flecked with the canoes of Indians, bound on some hunting or fishing or fighting expedition; and in 1635 a picturesque French trader—such a one of gentle birth, gift of leadership, and bold, adventurous spirit, as Sir Walter Scott might have loved to portray—built a huge wooden castle, bastioned and palisaded, on the banks of the St. John. There was enacted a fierce, confused drama, in which Indians and priests and rival gentlemen-traders took part; nor did it want a heroine, and to this day the noble courage and tragic end of Lady La Tour—wife of the lord of the castle—fascinate the imagination of every student of the annals of old Acadia.

In La Tour's lifetime an expedition sent out by Oliver Cromwell captured the fort on the St. John, and for some fifteen years the English held the river, restoring it to France by the Treaty of Breda. After that, great grants were made to French seigniors, but they contented themselves with trading with the Indians instead of improving the land, and the French settlements in what is now New Brunswick were of little account till after the expulsion of the Acadians from Nova Scotia in 1755.

To-day the descendants of French colonists of different periods number something over eighty thousand. About 1762 some families from New England settled at Maugerville, Sheffield, and Gagetown, and hither in the Revolutionary time came emissaries from the American "patriots," only just failing in the attempt to bring the St. John country under the "Stars and Stripes." But they did fail, and along the banks of the river there settled a few years later a host of the defeated, but not subdued, Americans, who held that true liberty was still possible within the circle of the British Empire.

These set to work with energy to tame the wilderness, and build the new British state of New Brunswick; and still all along the river and in many another district of the province are to be found their descendants, bearing the old names written a century and a quarter ago on the muster-rolls of the Loyalists. Hardships they had to endure in plenty, but they were happy at least in the fact that their country of refuge was a land richly blessed of nature. In fact, it has been calculated that New Brunswick could well support seventeen times her present population, which is about equal to that of the city of Bristol.

The three chief industries of the province are farming, fishing and lumbering. Masts were the first article of export, and for years the people almost lived by the timber trade. Even not very long ago this industry brought $10,000,000 (nearly £2,000,000) into the province yearly, of which one-third was paid out in wages;

and upon its prosperity depends the well-being of many not directly engaged in it. Since the introduction of iron vessels, the dependent industry of shipbuilding has declined, but new uses are continually being discovered for wood, increasing the value of all sources of supply. These have been recklessly reduced by greed, blunders and largely preventible accidents, but New Brunswick still possesses noble forests, and, perhaps, since the new day of deliberate "conservation" has dawned, may continue to possess them indefinitely.

The provincial government owns over 10,000 square miles of forest; but the greater part of this has been rented upon certain conditions for the cutting of timber, and the rents and dues thus collected bring in a considerable revenue to the public coffers. In 1906 it amounted to $250,000 (£50,000). Originally almost the whole of the province was covered with magnificent trees. For long, white pine was the only wood valued for export, and now little pine remains; but since the manufacture of paper from pulpwood began, a new value has been put upon the once despised spruce which, it has been said, grows in New Brunswick "like a weed," on lands where farmers would be predestined to failure. Nowadays, however, immigrants are not permitted to settle on such lands, for it is realized that their doing so will be of benefit neither to themselves nor to the province.

Spruce is exported as "deals" and boards, and is used for railway sleepers, fence posts, and building materials, as well as for pulpwood; but fir, tamarac, maple, elm, birch, ash, butternut, poplar and hemlock also abound, and serve many useful purposes.

One great advantage of New Brunswick as a lumbering region is that its rivers everywhere form excellent waterways, down which the logs can be "driven" to market. The St. John and its tributaries drain nearly one-half of the province, and the Miramichi has a "watershed embracing about five thousand square miles." Most of the forest exports go to Great Britain.

The lumbermen work in gangs of fifty or more, living in log camps built in the forests. The work is heavy, the life is rough, and accidents are somewhat frequent. For instance, when the logs going down stream get caught at some point and form a "jam," it is often a risky business to "break" it; but work in the woods is healthy, and the lumbermen are well fed. In fact, the cook in a lumber camp is a most important functionary.

Fishing is another old industry in New Brunswick, which has a sea-coast of about six hundred miles. Considerably over twenty thousand persons, including lobster canners, are employed. In 1909-10 the herring fishery proved most valuable of all. Next in order came the catches of lobsters, sardines (said to be equal to the Norwegian sardines), smelts (of which enormous numbers are caught in the Gulf of St. Lawrence), cod and salmon, which are exported fresh and frozen, smoked, salted or pickled. A variety of other fish are taken in smaller quantities.

Owing to ice the Gulf fisheries cease during the winter, but those of the Bay of Fundy are carried on all the year round. The old-time oyster fishery has suffered here, as in the neighbouring provinces; but steps are being taken to preserve and increase the productiveness of the fisheries, as of the forests, and to educate the fishermen. With the latter object, the Dominion government a few years ago brought to Canada "a Scottish expert," in the curing of herrings, "with a steam trawler and crew complete," and with a view to the former they established several hatcheries of young salmon and lobsters, from which 122,000,000 of the last-named were distributed in a single season.

In addition to these commercial fisheries, New Brunswick finds a source of profit, as well as pleasure, in her trout streams and salmon rivers, which attract hundreds of anglers and holiday-makers to the province, as the vast woods of the interior, stretching through a district eighty miles wide by a hundred long, bring in sportsmen in search of red deer, moose, caribou and wild fowl. This region, too, is the haunt of many valuable fur-bearing animals. The game laws aim at preserving the supply of game, and outsiders have to pay twenty-five times as much as residents for a hunter's licence, though in both cases the number of animals that may be killed is strictly limited. The province annually reaps a considerable harvest from licence fees, whilst the settlers in the wild districts to which the hunters go find the profits of the tourist trade a very welcome addition to incomes which are usually somewhat meagre.

There is not much mining, and of manufactures many depend on wood as their raw material. There are consequently many saw mills, pulp and paper mills, furniture and carriage factories. But this province, by the sea, is in a position to obtain readily and cheaply raw materials from other lands, such as cotton from the Southern States and sugar from the West Indies, so she has several cotton mills and "candy factories." Other manufactures that may be mentioned are those of boots and shoes, nails and other ironware, brass goods, soap and woollen cloths. Finally, in 1911, there were in operation twenty-four cheese factories and sixteen creameries, which bring us back all the way round the circle to agriculture, the most important industry of all.

Throughout New Brunswick there is much excellent land, suited for different purposes. Like Nova Scotia, the province has its salt marshes and dyked lands on the Bay of Fundy, and its "intervales" along the rivers, both famous for their enormous crops of hay. It has, too, districts as well adapted, it is said, for the culture of apples, as the Annapolis valley itself. In fact it, also, is a mixed farming region, where grains of all kinds will grow; where one man pins his faith to dairying; another urges the profits to be made from sheep or poultry or pigs; and a third points triumphantly to his enormous and excellent crops of potatoes. The fact is that practically every branch of agriculture could be made far more productive with better methods and more labourers, even on the farms now being worked—to say nothing of the land that might be cultivated, and is not, at present, for want of population.

The consequence is that while New Brunswick has a ready welcome for good workers—especially those ready to labour with their hands, and having enough in their pockets to tide over the time of seeking for the right niches—the people she wants above all are people to till her fertile soil.

1. HAYING IN NEW BRUNSWICK.

2. A FARM NEAR EVANDALE (EVANDALE FARM, NEW BRUNSWICK).

3. LUMBERING ON THE ST. JOHN RIVER.

One vast advantage the modern settler on the land has over the old-time pioneer. He will find it easy to get good prices for his produce, either in the local markets or in the more distant but still (owing to railways and steamship lines) easily accessible ones of other provinces or countries.

In common with the other Maritime Provinces, New Brunswick appears to have been somewhat overlooked as a field for immigration from the British Isles, perhaps because, in spite of its possessing seaports of its own, the general line of travel has been by Montreal or New York, or possibly because these provinces have been slow to advertise themselves. "Why did we never hear anything about New Brunswick when we were making inquiries about coming to Canada?" asked a lady, whose settlement with her family in Ontario thirty years ago was due to the excellent report of that province made by a number of Scottish farmers. "If we had only known what a good country it is," she added, "I daresay we might have stopped there, because it is so much nearer England."

Nearness to the British Isles is one incontrovertible advantage for settlers leaving behind them friends in the old land; and I must say that the part of New Brunswick that I know best—that is the sunny valley of the St. John—has a pleasantly homelike look to eyes accustomed to England's green hills and well-tilled fields. The sweeping lines of the low hills, the freshness of the mighty river, the great green woods massed here and there, the shady elms and willows of the little capital, the comfortable-looking farmhouses dotted along the slopes, all have a friendly familiar look of quiet content.

But I would not imply that this province is devoid of life and energy. The commercial capital, St. John (and there are many smaller towns like it), is much alive and "up-to-date," with its good railway connections and its numerous steamships plying both to American and British ports, and it will be still more busy when its great dry docks and shipbuilding plant are finished. St. John is the Atlantic terminus of the Canadian Pacific Railway, which takes a short cut to Montreal across a corner of the State of Maine, and of one of the two great branches into which the Intercolonial Railway divides. The new National Transcontinental Railway has its Atlantic terminus at Moncton; and altogether it is said that New Brunswick has more miles of railway in proportion to its population than any other country in the world. The province has about thirteen thousand miles of roads, but these generally stand in need of improvement. Of course the numerous rivers necessitate a large number of bridges; and there are nearly four thousand, ranging in type from the quaint old covered bridge, looking like a barn with its ends knocked out, to the great modern erection of steel. The capital, Fredericton, has a bridge about half a mile long, but a few miles higher upstream the St. John is crossed by a primitive-looking ferry.

In some districts population is much scattered. In others the people are "comfortably close together"; but everywhere there is ample room for more people. In fact, there is still land to be had, on certain conditions, for the asking, or "improved farms" may be bought at low prices. Many of these are very good farms; but a few years since the local markets were comparatively poor, work was scarce, and the young people went west or south or to the cities—it is the same story as in Nova

Scotia—in search of better opportunities.

With regard to the "free grants," ten thousand acres have been laid out, in Restigouche county, in hundred-acre lots, and to obtain a title to one of these, the applicant must pay a fee of $5 (about £1) for surveying, reside on the land for three years, clear four acres, build a small house, and do $30 (£6) worth of labour on the roads, or pay an additional $20 (£4) in cash. Besides these free grants, the government has opened to settlement the Blue Bell Tract in Victoria county, between the C.P.R. and the St. John river, on the one side, and the new Transcontinental Railway on the other. This district, watered by the Tobique river, is "a rolling upland, covered with a fine growth of trees, free from underbrush." Here hundred-acre lots, on a colonization road, are offered for sale at $1 the acre, one-fourth of the money to be paid on taking possession, and the remainder in four equal instalments.

For settlers with a little more capital, the government of New Brunswick has another proposition. A year or two ago a "Farm Settlement Board" of three commissioners was established by Act of Parliament, for the purpose of buying and improving suitable lands, erecting houses and farm buildings upon them, and selling them again to *bonâ fide* settlers upon easy terms, at cost price. The payment for these may be spread over ten years, and in special cases the Board is empowered to give two years' further grace; but the title "remains in the Board" till all payments have been made. (For addresses of persons from whom information may be obtained, see Appendix, Note A, page 160.)

In the ordinary way, farms may be bought in New Brunswick from $10 (£2) to $25 (£5) the acre, according to their size, the character of the soil, the condition of the buildings, their nearness to church, school and markets, and the proportion of land under cultivation. Most farmers in the province own the lands they occupy.

Not every man who might do well on an improved farm is suited to the "roughing it" involved in clearing a free grant; but if a newcomer, with little or no capital, is content to work for a time on wages, he can often put by enough to enable him to start to buy a farm for himself. Wages for a good man run from $10 (£2) or $15 (£3) monthly in the winter months to $20 (£4) in the summer, with board and lodging for a single man and a free house for a married one. Sometimes the farmers hire men only for the busy season, but work may often be obtained by a strong man in the lumber camps, even though he may not have had experience of the work. Of course it means hard, long, patient work to obtain success by such means; but the opportunities in New Brunswick are sufficiently great to ensure that thrift and industry usually have their reward.

The right of every child to a good sound education is recognized in New Brunswick, though in some of the country districts the salaries offered are so small that it is difficult to obtain fully qualified teachers. In this province also, the consolidated school has been tried with success. There is provision for a grammar school in every county, and at Fredericton (which is also the seat of the Provincial University) there is a Normal Training and a Model School for teachers.

The newcomer to New Brunswick may obtain much useful information as to the classes of fruit and stock likely to do well in his particular district, and advice on kindred subjects, if he chooses to write to the Department of Agriculture at Ottawa. Or, if he wishes to obtain instructions from specialists in bee-keeping, poultry-raising or apple-growing, he may write to the provinicial government at Fredericton. In 1904, by the way, the latter began, through experts, the planting and direction of "illustration orchards" in different districts. These are managed on an interesting plan of co-operation, the government supplying the young trees and the expert knowledge, and the farmer supplying the labour and the land and reaping the fruit, on condition that for ten years "he will cultivate and care for the orchard in accordance with the directions of the Department of Agriculture." The newcomer may also gain much help from his neighbours, especially if he joins the Agricultural Association of his district and shows willingness to make himself one with them generally.

These and other associations formed for serious purposes, as well as the churches, have a great social value in sparsely settled districts; but though the farmers and their families are generally industrious they do not believe in all work and no play, and in the winter especially they find some time for visiting and recreation.

At present by far the greater proportion of the people are natives of the province, chiefly of British stock. Of the remainder, some thousands were born in the British Isles, and several thousands more have come in from the United States. More than a quarter of the people are French; there are also a number of Germans, Dutch, Scandinavians and other foreigners.

In religion more than a third of the people are Roman Catholics; but this body is surpassed in number of church buildings both by the Baptists and the Methodists. Of Protestant denominations, the Baptists are strongest, then follow the Anglicans, Presbyterians and the Methodists. Of course there is no "established church" here, nor in any part of Canada; and the chaplain of the legislative assembly (New Brunswick has only a single chamber), who opens the proceedings with prayer, is chosen in rotation from the Baptists, Anglicans, Presbyterians and Methodists.

VIII

PRINCE EDWARD ISLAND

THIS, by far the smallest of the Canadian provinces, seems to exercise a peculiar charm on all who visit or dwell within it. "Abegweit"—"Rest on the Wave"—was the poetic name bestowed upon it by its Indian inhabitants; and rugged Jacques Cartier, the Breton explorer, described the country in glowing terms as "the most beautiful it is possible to see . . . full of beautiful trees and meadows . . . of pease, white and red gooseberries, strawberries, blackberries and wild grain like rye," and having "the best temperature it is possible to see."

In shape Prince Edward Island bears some resemblance to a crescent with the two horns turned northwards, and the outer curve lying from nine to fifteen miles away from the corresponding curve of the mainland shores of New Brunswick and Nova Scotia. Its greatest length is about one hundred and forty miles, and its greatest breadth thirty-four miles, but its shores are so deeply indented with bays and inlets that the distance between water and water is in places only two miles.

Its soil is peculiarly fertile; and compared with the other provinces—all of which have large stretches of wild land, either uncultivated or uncultivable—it may well claim the title of the "Garden of the Gulf," for 86 per cent. of its surface is occupied by farms, and very little of the remaining 14 per cent. is actually worthless for agriculture.

It has no mountains or wild, rugged hills, no great forests, and of course no great rivers; but the land is pleasantly undulating, vegetation is usually richly green, contrasting with soil of a warm reddish hue, with glints of shining water, or with lines of snowy breakers, roaring on the sands. In general the character of the scenery is mild and gentle and smiling; with a glad wealth of colour when the orchards are breaking into bloom, or when the first touch of frost is kindling a magic glow amongst the maples and sumach trees. But the wildly-beating surf on the reefs of the north shore forbids that even here nature's majesty and strength and terror should be forgotten.

The climate is milder than that of the mainland near by, neither so sharply cold in winter nor so fiercely hot in summer, though all writers have praise for the "Island's" clear blue skies and plenitude of sunlight.

Prince Edward Island is reached by steamers from Point du Chêne in New Brunswick to Summerside; and from Pictou in Nova Scotia to Charlottetown; or from Pictou to Georgetown, when the strait is full of ice. Strongly-built ice-breaking steamers, however, usually manage to keep open communication with the capital of the little province; and in winter there is an "ice-boat service," by which the adventurous can cross from Cape Tormentine to Cape Traverse. The ice-boat is contrived to travel either in water or on the ice by means of "twin keels," which in case of necessity serve as "runners."

The people, however, have for long demanded improved means of communication with the mainland, and at last a "car-ferry" steamer (powerful enough to force its way through the worst ice) is to be constructed to connect the railway on the island with the Intercolonial line on the mainland. Both are owned by the Dominion government. "The island railway is of a narrow gauge, but it is to be changed this year to the standard gauge (4 ft. 8½ ins.) of the Canadian and American lines." When this is done, Prince Edward Island will be very happily situated in the matter of transportation service, for into her three counties, all with easy water-communication, is packed a well-branched railway line of two hundred and sixty miles.

Prince Edward Island was first called the Island of St. John, but historians are not agreed as to who bestowed this name upon "the right little, tight little island." Some people think it was John Cabot; some Samuel Champlain; but, at any rate, it bore the name from the time its history began until 1799, when it was re-christened in honour of Queen Victoria's father. In 1663 it was granted by the "Company of New France" to a French naval officer, Doublet, and a few fishing stations were established. As late as 1728 it had only three hundred inhabitants; but after the deportation of the Acadians from Nova Scotia in 1755, a good many of these hapless people took refuge in the peaceful island. It was annexed by the British the year before the capture of Quebec, and was amongst the territories formally ceded to England by the Treaty of Paris in 1763.

In 1767 the soil of nearly the whole island was disposed of in one day to officers and other gentlemen, who agreed to settle the country, and, by paying small "quit-rents" for their lands, to provide for the cost of government. Small reservations were made for the support of churches and schools; but the plan, it may be said, was an utter failure, saddling the island for many years with a class of absentee landlords, who did practically nothing for the country. For more than a century the cultivators of the soil remained in the position of tenants.

In 1873, when the province agreed to enter into Confederation, the Dominion government granted $800,000 (£160,000) to aid in buying out the land-owners; but many would not sell, till an Act was passed in 1875 obliging them to sell at a fair price to the Provincial government, which in turn sold to the tenants.

Many years earlier, in 1851, the Islanders had secured responsible government. At that time the Parliament consisted of a Governor and Legislative Council, appointed by the Crown, and an elective Assembly. Later, the Council also was elected by owners of leasehold and freehold property worth $325 (£65) and over. Finally, in 1893, the unusual arrangement was made of amalgamating the two branches of the Legislature; and now fifteen councilmen, chosen by the property-owners, and fifteen assembly men, elected by the men of the Province, on a property qualification so low that scarcely any man is excluded, sit and vote together.

The legislature of Prince Edward Island, which first met in 1773, is housed in a fine old, grey stone building in Charlottetown, fronting on Queen Square, about which are other public buildings, including the Law Courts, the General Post Office, the Custom House, and the market building, which every Tuesday and Friday, when the country people come in to dispose of their produce, presents a very animated scene.

But to return to the government. The expenditure on the salaries of the Lieutenant-Governor, the cabinet ministers and the members of the assembly; the administration of justice; the support of schools and public works and some other charges amount to $420,000 (about £84,000). Three-fourths of this is met by the subsidy from the Federal government, and the remaining quarter is raised by provincial taxes, which are very low. The province is represented in the Dominion parliament by four senators, and four members of the House of Commons.

The population, despite the prosperity of the island, diminished by over nine thousand between 1901 and the next census year, 1911. It has been suggested that this was due in part to the "lure of the West," and perhaps in part to the fact that many of the people are descended from that race of wanderers and excellent pioneers, the Scotch. During the great migration of the American loyalists northward, the Island of St. John obtained a considerable addition to its population. These were of various races; but in 1803 Lord Selkirk brought out eight hundred Highland crofters, and after a short time of hardship these colonists settled down happily. Many of their descendants still dwell in the island.

There are a few manufacturing establishments at the capital—Charlottetown—and at others of its small centres of population, but chiefly of a description depending directly on the industries of fishing and farming.

The island is naturally a favourable place for fishermen. Its fisheries of cod, mackerel, herring, lobsters and oysters are important, the latter fishery being the most valuable of its kind in Canada. The "Malpeque oyster," from the bay so named, is widely famous, and the provincial government is taking steps "to extend and develop this industry by the replanting and cultivation of an area estimated at one hundred thousand acres."

The tourist trade is such an important branch of the island's industries that, in this connection, it is matter for congratulation that the summer visitors can find trout in the numerous streams and can enjoy sea-fishing from boats. As for game, moose and bears need not be looked for in the "Garden" province; but wild fowl are plentiful in the season.

After all, however, the soil is the chief source of wealth, and the island possesses "a fertilizer of singular value and potency" in the mussel or oyster mud found in vast quantities in all its bays and river mouths, and consisting of "the organic remains of countless generations of oysters, mussels, clams and other bivalves." This is a veritable "mine of wealth to the island," enriching the poorest soils, so that they grow excellent crops of clover, turnips and potatoes.

A FOX FARM IN PRINCE EDWARD ISLAND.

In times past the settlers of Prince Edward Island made the mistake—common in farming virgin soils—of continuing year after year to raise the same crop, without taking any measures to secure the continued fertility of the soil. Happily, through private enterprise and government encouragement, more scientific methods are coming into fashion, and the farmers are going extensively into dairying. In consequence, many farms have gone up 50 per cent. in value and productiveness during the past two decades; and, in the last census, little Prince Edward Island could point with pardonable pride to a much greater product from her dairy factories than could be shown by either of the far larger provinces of Nova Scotia and New Brunswick.

In proportion to size this province has the largest population of any, but there is room still for many a good farmer. It is not a land of free grants, but there are farms for sale at reasonable prices which could be farmed to great advantage by men with a little capital, trained in good English methods. Of course the prices depend on situation and worth of buildings, as well as on the quality of the land, but farms of different sizes ranging from ten to two hundred and fifty acres may be bought at from about £2 the acre (in the case of good-sized farms) to £16 the acre.

In Prince Edward Island such a large proportion of the people are farmers that their importance to the community is recognized more readily than where the mercantile classes predominate and have the ear of the government. Great efforts are now being made to give an education in the public schools suited to the needs of the rural population. At the Teachers' College and Normal School in Charlottetown courses of lectures are given in agriculture. At several places school gardens have been introduced with good results, and in others one "consolidated school," with different teachers for different classes, has taken the place of six ordinary schools, the children being taken to and from the centre in vans. Steps have also been taken to arrange for better salaries for teachers.

The farmers and their families work hard, but usually find some time for reading, music, or other recreations, and social gatherings, especially in the "slack" winter season, and as a rule they live well. They are rarely addicted to indulgence in any liquor stronger than tea. In fact, the sale of intoxicants, unless prescribed by a doctor, is prohibited in Prince Edward Island, and, though the law may be sometimes evaded, the consumption of strong drink is much less than it was a generation ago.

There are many churches in Prince Edward Island. Considerably over one-third of the people belong to the church of Rome, and of the Protestant denominations the Presbyterians are much the strongest. The people support their own churches, largely by congregational subscriptions, supplemented in poor districts by grants from the "Mission Funds" of the particular religious body. Of course the churches are a very important factor in the social as well as the religious life of the people. In this connection, societies and organizations, such as the "Sons of Temperance" and the "Foresters," are also of importance.

There is a demand in Prince Edward Island for farm workers, and though the wages are not quite so high as in some parts of Canada, it has the advantage for

British immigrants of being nearer to England, and of conditions more closely resembling those of the "Old Country." Wages for an experienced man, with board and lodging, range from $12 (£2 8s.) a month in the winter to $16 (£3 4s.) a month through the busy season, of about eight months; a married man can often obtain a cottage rent free.

In any notice of Prince Edward Island one industry must by no means be forgotten. This is the breeding of black foxes, of which the fur is immensely valuable. It began in 1896, when a man living in Tignish bought three black foxes caught near Bedeque for $300 (£60); but the price of a good pair has now gone up to $20,000 (£4,000). Black foxes have been imported from Labrador, and now "fox ranches" in the island can be counted by hundreds. In 1911 the value of this curious branch of stock-raising was estimated at $2,000,000. In the early part of 1913 the capital invested, by some six thousand shareholders, reached $6,000,000. In that year, on the opening of the Provincial Legislature, the industry was mentioned in the "speech from the throne," and during the session forty new companies were incorporated.

IX

QUEBEC AND ITS EASTERN TOWNSHIPS

ALIKE in its scenery and its history, Quebec, which was the first "Canada," is one of the most picturesque provinces of the Dominion.

In the year 1534, the Breton mariner, Jacques Cartier, sailed up the St. Lawrence till he could see land on both sides. Next year he came again with three well-appointed vessels (none over one hundred and twenty tons burden) to colonize and to trade. It was he who called a small bay, in which his vessels lay upon the Saint's day, St. Lawrence, a name afterwards extended to the "Great River of Canada," and to the gulf into which it flows. It was he, too, who, penetrating later in the year far up the river, bestowed the title of "Mont Royale"—now anglicized to Montreal—upon the "Mountain" beneath which, over a century later, the devout and gallant Maisonneuve began the settlement destined to grow into Canada's greatest city. Cartier himself spent one winter at the point where the St. Charles enters the St. Lawrence, near the Indian village of Stadacona.

But a greater man than he was to have the honour of founding Quebec. Cartier's men suffered horribly from the cold and from scurvy, against which ills they did not know how properly to protect themselves, and in the spring the remnant of the company sailed for home, carrying off with them the chief, Donnacona, and nine other Indians. Two or three other attempts to establish French settlements on the St. Lawrence were made by Cartier, Roberval and La Roche, but it was not till 1608 that Champlain at last "well and truly laid" the foundations of Quebec.

Of his company also two-thirds died, during the first winter, of scurvy, but this time the French were there to stay, and for a century and a-half Quebec was both the head and heart of Canada.

The proud little city, clinging to and climbing upon the rock, was the seat of the French rulers, the centre of the colony which—despite government restrictions, despite its own early limitations as a mere trading post and mission station, despite the terrible hostility of the Iroquois and the frequent attacks of the English, despite the "wanderlust" of its own more energetic sons, which led to a dissipation of the strength of New France as a whole—struck its roots so deep into the soil, that through all vicissitudes it has preserved to this day its own peculiar type of civilization.

To old Quebec, Canadians, whether of French or British descent, turn with much the same feeling that thrills an English heart at the thought of Westminster Abbey. There is something strangely satisfying in the beauty of rock and river, of distant blue hills and shining water, of ancient gabled roofs, grey walls, and antique, harmless-looking cannon; something stirring in memories of the heroes of two races, which mingle at Quebec; and inspiring for the future in the peaceful outcome of the grim struggles of the past.

But if one would really learn to know the French-Canadians of to-day, he must not be content to observe only the brisk city men in their offices and stores, nor the dainty little maidens who on Sundays promenade in gay attire on Dufferin Terrace, before that great modern hotel, the "Château Frontenac." He must visit the markets, where the country people drive their trade in eggs and butter, poultry and small pink pigs, knitted goods and queer homegrown tobacco. He must go into the country beyond and around Quebec, and penetrate, if possible, into the quaint little wooden or stone houses, where all kinds of old-world employments are carried on by the busy mothers of families, which not infrequently number ten or a dozen children.

The French-Canadians generally are credited with being a thrifty, industrious folk, but it looks to an outsider as if the women do the heavier share of the work, for, not content with those tasks of sweeping and cleaning, cooking and milking, spinning and sewing, nursing the babies and all the house mothers' other miscellaneous duties, the women, in their flat, black mushroom hats, are constantly seen with the men, hoeing root-crops or working in the hay-fields.

The "habitants," as the country folk call themselves, are a conservative people, following customs much the same as those of their ancestors who first settled in Canada. But the conditions under which they live are greatly changed. During the last years of the French régime, Canada was neglected by her mother-land, and amongst the officials sent out to govern the country were not a few bent on enriching themselves at any cost. The last Intendant of New France—an official charged with the administration of justice, and the management of the finances of the colony—was a clever scoundrel named Bigot, and his devices for diverting the public funds to his own pockets, and squeezing all manner of corrupt profits from the people, were endless and shameless. In those days there was no such thing as municipal government in Canada, and the affairs of the settlement were managed chiefly by the Intendant; and appeals to the king—three thousand miles away—were difficult and often ineffective.

The system of land tenure in New France has been described as "a mild form of feudalism." The king gave large grants of land under certain conditions to a number of seigneurs, usually of good family, who in turn made grants to tenants or "censitaires," who were expected to clear and farm the lands, paying to the seigneur a small rent, sometimes in money, oftener in kind. The seigneur might also demand a certain portion of the fish caught by his tenants, and require them to use, and pay for the use of, his mill and his oven. But if they fulfilled the stipulated conditions, they could not be dispossessed.

VIEW OF QUEBEC FROM THE RIVER, SHOWING CITADEL.

No steps were taken till the nineteenth century to relieve the habitants of the burdens of seigneurial tenure. In fact, the rents had become heavier; but, in 1854, an Act of Parliament was passed abolishing the feudal rights and duties, and granting compensation to the seigneurs. Not all the tenants took advantage of this measure, and in some instances the annual rent is still paid.

But the English conquest was the beginning of a new era of freedom for the French-Canadians. As one of the race, the well-known writer, Mr. Benjamin Sulte, says, it "abolished the paper money of the old régime, and substituted cash payments; enabled the habitants, who formed nine-tenths of the population at the time, to purchase where they pleased and what they pleased, instead of being obliged to go to the company's or government store; gave greater freedom for trade and abolished unjust monopolies; and paved the way for those legislative measures which, at a subsequent date, conferred local self-government and schools upon the French subjects of Great Britain."

At first, indeed, there was some confusion in the province as to whether the French or English system of law was in force, but by the Quebec Act, enacted in 1774, the French laws regarding property and civil rights were definitely restored to Canada, and the free exercise of their religion was secured to the adherents of the Roman Catholic church. A few years later, in 1792, it was determined that in the parliament of Lower Canada both the French and English languages might be used. This arrangement was naturally continued when the provinces of Upper and Lower Canada were united, and is still in force in the Dominion Parliament.

The Provincial Legislature of Quebec has two chambers: a Council of twenty-four members, appointed for life; and an elective Assembly of seventy-four members.

Taxes are light. The revenue of the province is derived chiefly from the subsidy paid by the Dominion; from the sales and leases of the crown lands; and from fees for licences of various kinds. Between March, 1905, and June, 1910, the provincial debt was reduced by over $9,000,000.

Quebec, with the recent addition of Ungava (of which the value cannot yet be estimated), now stretches on the north to Hudson Strait, and is the largest province of the Dominion, containing nearly 707,000 square miles, or five times the area of the United Kingdom. Even the older part of the province is still largely undeveloped, and will remain so till there are vast additions to the population.

The climate is healthy, though admittedly cold in winter. "During the four coldest months of the year," I quote from an official publication, "the average temperature is 15 degrees Fahrenheit in December, 10 in January, 10 to 15 in February, and 20 to 25 in March. There are some days when the mercury drops as low as 20 to 30 degrees below zero, but the atmosphere is so dry that but little discomfort is experienced, even by those who indulge in winter sports in the coldest weather."

There is no question that the dryness of the atmosphere makes an immense difference in the extent to which one feels the cold, and though I cannot speak from experience of a Quebec winter, I know that many people do prefer the crisp cold of the Dominion's oldest province to a damper and milder climate.

MONTMORENCY FALLS, A WATER-POWER, QUEBEC PROVINCE.

Quebec has the advantage of having plenty of snow, which makes winter travelling easy and delightful. It also "protects the grass and autumn-sown grain from damage by frost, and, as in England, tulips and crocuses which have remained in the ground all winter, push their green shoots through the disappearing snowbanks in the early spring."

Of course, however, one must dress suitably to the weather. Warm caps, coats, gloves and overshoes are necessary, especially for driving, in Lower Canada; the "habitants" wear blanket coats, girt round the waist with a coloured sash, and woollen caps which can be pulled down over the ears and neck—a costume which is at once so sensible and so picturesque, that a modification of it has been adopted nearly all over Canada for the little folk and by their elder brothers and sisters for snow-shoeing and ski-ing.

But Quebec is not only a land of ice-palaces and deep snow. It has its hot months as well as its cold ones, and often the latter follow the former so quickly that "the rapidity of vegetation is marvellous. Peas and beans ripen six weeks after being sown. The thermometer sometimes registers 70 degrees and over in the month of May; and in the early part of July, 1911, it stood at over 80 in the shade at Quebec for several days together." When the writer first set foot in Montreal, it was the second week in September, and coming in from the sea, in a season when the icebergs had been adrift in large numbers, it would have seemed that summer still reigned, had it not been for such a wealth of fruit—pears, apples, peaches, grapes—everywhere in evidence, as only autumn can produce.

In population, Quebec comes second to Ontario. The census of 1911 showed a total of nearly two million three thousand persons, of whom the males outnumbered the females by almost twenty thousand; and the gain during the preceding decade was greater than in any other eastern province. Four-fifths of the people in Quebec are French-speaking, and of these 70 per cent. live in villages and rural districts.

Quebec is a beautiful province of mountain and valley, forest, lake and river. It was along the rivers and the coasts of the gulf that its settlement first began. In fact, it was the St. Lawrence that made New France; yet even to-day there is only a fringe of settlement on its northern shore, backed by the Laurentide mountains, and beyond those is the vast scarcely explored wilderness. But the villages continue up the east bank of the Ottawa; and, south of the St. Lawrence, as far east as Rimouski, there is a fairly well-peopled section of country.

The pioneer settlers, like the redmen, at first used the graceful bark canoes as their chief means of conveyance. These could be carried with ease over the "portages" necessitated by the numerous rapids, but when the settlers began to build larger boats, they were soon obliged to improve the navigation of the inland waterways by constructing canals, a work that has been going on for over a century, and is likely long to continue.

Large vessels could always go up to Quebec, and vessels of five hundred or six hundred tons could reach Montreal. But in 1844 the work of cutting a deeper channel was begun. Thirty shoals had to be cut through, and during the next sixty years nearly six million dollars, over a million pounds, was expended, with the result that there is now a "submerged canal, thirty feet deep and 500 feet wide," up which, as it is well lighted, great ships can come by night as well as day. At Montreal, which is nearly a hundred miles above tidal influence, there arrived in 1850 two hundred and ten small vessels; but in 1912 there came seven hundred and thirty-six ocean liners, with a tonnage over fifty times as great as that of 1850.

Several of the tributaries of the St. Lawrence, including the Ottawa, the St. Maurice and the Saguenay, are navigable for great distances, and Quebec is a province of numerous and beautiful waterfalls, upon which the business man gazes, with calculations of the immense "power" available for the manufactures of to-day or to-morrow. In manufactures, Quebec comes next after Ontario. High up in the list of her industrial products come those of which the raw material is obtained from forest or farm, such as lumber and paper, butter and cheese, but it contains also iron goods, boots and shoes, fur garments, clothing, cottons, cigars, etc., etc.

Montreal, with a population of about half a million, is the largest city of the Dominion, and a great industrial centre. Something has been said already of its importance as a port for ocean steamers, but it has also connections by the inland waterways with Lake Superior. In addition, it is the greatest railway centre of Canada. Here both the Canadian Pacific and the Grand Trunk systems have their headquarters, whilst a number of smaller lines give connection with the United States.

In point of numbers, picturesque old Quebec comes a long way behind its slightly younger sister, Montreal, but the former also has a fine port. In the summer it is the point where immigrants, travelling third-class by the St. Lawrence route, disembark to go to their various destinations by rail. Its chief industries are connected with leather and wood. It has also several cotton factories. Other industrial centres are Hull, with wood-working establishments, ranging from saw mills to match factories; Sherbrooke, where the first cotton factory in Canada was opened in 1844; St. Hyacinthe, Three Rivers, Sorel and Valleyfield.

The forests are one of the chief assets of Quebec. Leaving out of account the recently-annexed northern regions, eighty million acres, estimated to be worth $450,000,000, are still the absolute property of the province; but forty-five million acres have been leased to lumbermen and six million acres are in private hands. Not very long ago a government "forestry service" was established for the protection of the existing forests and the replanting of "wild and denuded lands." In 1905 the Laurentides National Park, designed especially for the preservation of fish and game, was Quebec's only forest reserve. Now ten reserves, comprising 165,000 square miles, have been set apart to be held for the benefit of the whole population and of posterity. The immense value of such reserves may be guessed at from the fact that even under the old haphazard system, the timber limits brought into the provincial coffers during a period of about forty-five years a sum of nearly $29,000,000 (£5,800,000).

The lumber industry gives employment, during the winter months, when most other work is slack, to over twenty thousand men, in addition to the thousands of log-drivers required every spring to take the season's cut down the rivers to market. Much of the government forests (chiefly of pulpwood) have been inaccessible, but the construction of the Transcontinental Railway, which passes through these forests, is adding immensely to their value, and, whenever they are opened to lumbering operations, numerous pulp and paper mills are likely to be erected. In 1912 the province already had twenty-eight of these mills.

Quebec possesses much mineral wealth, but it is little developed as yet, though as long ago as the first half of the eighteenth century a small blast furnace, for smelting bog iron ore with charcoal, was established at Three Rivers. Coal has not yet been discovered in Quebec, but the vast deposits of peat may, in a measure, supply its place. Copper and gold have been produced in a small way, and there are good building stones, slates and materials from which cement, brick, tiles and pottery can be made. But the mineral product of first value, reaching considerably over $3,000,000 (£600,000) in 1911, is asbestos. In that year four-fifths of the world's whole product came from Quebec. The deposits, of immense extent, lie in the "Eastern Townships," about seventy-five miles south of Quebec city, and were discovered in 1878, when the Quebec Central Railway was being constructed.

The fisheries of the province, both from the commercial and sportsman's standpoint, are valuable. The former in 1909-10 gave employment with the canneries, to nearly twelve thousand persons and brought in nearly $2,000,000 (£400,000), cod, lobsters and bait yielding the largest contributions to this sum. An almost equal amount, it was estimated, was spent by sportsmen and anglers who came to the forests; and much of this money fortunately finds its way to the settlers (generally poor) of districts not well adapted to agriculture. In the regions north of the St. Lawrence and in the Canadian Labrador, bears, wolves, beavers and other wild animals abound to this day, and the fur trade, once the chief support of New France, still brings about $1,000,000 (£200,000) annually into the province.

Now agriculture holds the first place, and the farmers of Quebec, represented in 1617 by one solitary tiller of the soil, Louis Hébert, have become a great army. Enough has been said, I think, to show that Quebec has a variety of opportunities to offer to strong and capable and industrious immigrants; but perhaps the best of these are in agriculture. In different districts are millions of acres of good land still wild and uncultivated. Of these, six and a quarter millions have been surveyed and divided into farm lots of one hundred acres each, and these are almost given away to *bonâ fide* settlers, on condition of their clearing a few acres and erecting a small house, barn and stable within five years. The price charged is at the rate of from 20 cents (10*d.*) to 60 cents (2*s.* 6*d.*) an acre, payable in five instalments.

If the newcomer shrinks from the idea of taking up one of these uncleared farms, there are plenty of more or less "improved farms" to be bought at prices varying widely in different districts and under different circumstances.

1. A DAIRY FARM NEAR SHERBROOKE, QUEBEC.

2. GOVERNMENT DEMONSTRATION FARM IN THE EASTERN TOWNSHIPS, AT KNOWLTON—QUEBEC.

To British farmers with a little capital or to farm labourers from the United Kingdom, the beautiful district south of the St. Lawrence, known as the "Eastern Townships," has been warmly recommended as a region where conditions more nearly resemble those of the "Old Country" than most parts of this new land. It was first settled by Loyalists from the revolted American colonies, towards the close of the eighteenth century. These earliest comers had to endure many hardships, but now the whole district is peculiarly prosperous, possessing not only good farms, but a considerable number of manufacturing and industrial establishments, including the asbestos quarries already mentioned.

Most of the counties of Quebec are divided into "parishes," but the Loyalists had been accustomed to "townships" in the land from which they came, hence "the Eastern Townships," comprising an area of about four and a half million acres, and including the eleven counties of Brome, Compton, Drummond and Arthabaska, Megantic, Missisquoi, Richmond and Wolfe, Shefford, Sherbrooke and Stanstead. Of this district, Sherbrooke, which in 1911 had seventeen thousand inhabitants, may be counted the capital. It is one hundred and twenty-five miles south of Quebec, and being in a central situation is the distributing point for immigrants bound for the "Townships."

The soil of this region is generally fertile, and the climate is by no means a bad one either for the human being or for the products of his fields. In latitude these counties correspond with the northern portion of Italy; but, though "Green Yules" are not unknown, someone has rather happily described the winter as "decided" in its character, and usually the snow comes about the beginning of December, to lie two or three feet deep and make good sleighing for several months. The summer is also a "decided" one; and many a fruit and vegetable which will not ripen in the open air in England here comes to perfection. The inhabitants of the country think the climate peculiarly healthy, and the census reports bear out the assertion so far as to show that an unusually large number of people live to be eighty or ninety.

It must not be supposed that in these long-settled counties there remains any public land to be disposed of; but there are plenty of good farms, of from one hundred and fifty to three hundred acres, for sale at prices ranging from $2,000 (£400) to $8,000 (£1,600), and a considerable portion of the purchase money may always be borrowed on mortgage. That there are so many of these farms for sale is due, as in other parts of Eastern Canada, to the attraction of the West, and of the cities and of other professions than farming; but it is asserted that farming in this region of easy accessibility to good markets has never before been so profitable as it is now. For many products there is an excellent local demand. Moreover, "the Townships" are in easy reach of Montreal and of some of the cities of the United States, and are served by the Canadian Pacific Railway, by the Grand Trunk and other lines—736 miles in all. Prices of produce are now high, and (unfortunately for the consumer) seem likely to remain so even if the supplies should be very largely increased. That the productivity of this district could be more than doubled if the population were doubled is no doubt true, for, though compared to the population of Canada, as a whole (which has less than two persons to the square mile), the Eastern Townships (with about thirty-four persons to the square mile) are well peopled, the density of population even here is only about one-tenth of that of the United Kingdom.

There is generally a scarcity of farm labourers in the district, and a year ago it was said that several thousand experienced workers could get work at wages ranging from $10 (£2) to $35 (£7) the month, in addition to board and lodging, or a rent-free house. As for "Old Country" girls, able and willing to do housework, they can readily obtain places in the towns and villages at wages of from $10 to $20 the month, that is, at from £24 to £48 the year.

Owing to the fact that there is a demand in winter for men to work in the lumber camps of Quebec, and that the farming carried on in this district (and the province generally) is of the "mixed" type, there is a fair demand for men in winter as well as summer—a most important consideration in comparing wages and opportunities in different places.

Here, too, it is said that experience of farming gained in England stands the newcomer in good stead to an especial degree; but, of course, there are some differences. For instance, after dairying and live-stock raising, the making of maple sugar is a large source of revenue to Eastern Township farmers. The sharp night frosts and warm days of early spring in this region are favourable to the flow of sap, and the average farm has from six hundred to one thousand maples, and some farms have three or four thousand. In a good year the yield of sugar may be as much as 3 lbs. to a tree. This sells at about 8 cents the pound. But if a farmer is an adept at making syrup, his profits may be increased.

The Townships have an agent at Quebec to meet incoming steamers and to help new arrivals on their way; and within the last few years some five thousand British immigrants have settled in the district. Some have found work in the shops and mills of the towns, but most have gone to the farms, and here and there amongst the prosperous farmers of the district is one who could tell an interesting story of his arrival at Quebec with scarcely a penny and of his gradual climb up the ladder to a position of comfort.

By the way, there are plenty of churches of different denominations and schools and other social advantages which make life pleasant in the Townships, and probably for English-speaking people, especially for those who are Protestants, this part of Quebec will prove more homelike than any of the counties where the population is almost entirely French-speaking and Roman Catholic.

To return to the province in general, though it has still too many illiterates, there has been progress during the last few years in educational matters, and within seven years the government grant for this purpose was much more than doubled. Owing to the marked religious differences, there are two classes of public schools—the regular public schools and the "separate" schools of the minority, which may be Protestant in one district and Roman Catholic in another. The Roman Catholic and Protestant schools are represented, in the department of education, by French and English secretaries or deputy-heads, under the general "Superintendent of Public Instruction." In the different localities, school affairs are regulated by "commissioners" representing the religious majority, and "trustees" representing the minority. These are elected by the ratepayers, who pay school rates to the school board of their own religious faith.

Recently new technical schools have been opened in Quebec and Montreal, and the latter city now has a "School of Higher Commercial Studies." There are also Provincial Forestry and Veterinary Schools. Finally, there is the great Roman Catholic University of Laval, with branches in Quebec and Montreal, which is the outgrowth of a seminary founded in the seventeenth century by the first bishop of Canada; and the non-sectarian McGill University, which owes its foundation in 1814 to the bequest of a wealthy merchant of Montreal, but has since been enriched by benefactions from Lord Strathcona and others. It is said, indeed, to be the wealthiest of Canadian universities. It has a large number of departments, and is well equipped for research work in medicine, physics, engineering, and so forth. Women are admitted to its courses on equal terms with men. This university, by the way, owes much to the famous Nova Scotian geologist, Sir William Dawson, who was its principal for thirty-eight years, and during that time saw the number of its undergraduates increase from eighty to over a thousand.

FROM THE LOOK-OUT, MOUNT ROYAL, MONTREAL.

X

ONTARIO, ONCE "CANADA WEST"

WE come now to Ontario, in extent the second, but in certain respects the first, of the Canadian provinces. Not so large as Quebec, it yet comprises an area three times that of the British Isles, with a little to spare. To be more exact, the figures are 407,262 square miles, having recently been increased immensely by the addition of the new district of Patricia, to the north of its former limits; and now the outline of Ontario upon the map bears a rude resemblance to a great humpbacked whale. At present it is only the tail of the monster that has much population, and it is that portion of Ontario—the peninsula outlined by the Ottawa River, the St. Lawrence and the Great Lakes—with which the brief, interesting history of the portion of the Empire that began its existence as "Upper Canada" one hundred and twenty years since, has most to do.

Canadians, like their American cousins, are sometimes accused of worshipping mere bigness. This may or may not be true; but bigness is a factor of the situation in the Dominion from which one cannot get away. There is, I suppose, something fascinating to the imagination of the average mortal in the thought of leagues upon leagues of little-known, scarcely-explored wilderness, awaiting the coming of men, to be turned to unguessed uses in the service of humanity (sometimes unfortunately represented mainly by millionaires and the "big interests").

Enough at least is known of these vast spaces to render it practically certain that, when their day comes, they will prove to be of much value to man. Obstructions in the waterways of the early "voyageurs" now stand for "power" and progress. Trees, once regarded as little better than noxious weeds, now furnish the paper for this news-reading generation. Rocks that cost the railway companies vast expense and toil in blasting have proved mines of precious metals. The chill waters of Hudson Bay may yet furnish the tables of half a continent with fish; and lands, supposed to be too far north for any useful growth, are so bathed in sunshine during the long days of the brief northern summer that roots and grains are forced to swift perfection, and the harvest seems to tread on the heels of the sowing. What will the next few decades show even in Ontario? Who can say? But bigness means difficulty and toil and struggle, as well as opportunity; and what every province of Canada needs is a people not only numerous enough, but big enough to make something of themselves and of the country.

Upon the whole, Upper Canada began well with the stock of sturdy Loyalists who had dared in the "Thirteen Colonies" to try to stem the tide of revolution, and were cast out by their native land in very fear of their strength and their constancy. Then came settlers from the Motherlands—English, Scotch and Irish (the latter arriving by the thousand during the first half of the nineteenth century at different times of sore distress in the Emerald Isle)—and though amongst these were wastrels and ne'er-do-wells and weaklings, the majority were men and women strong enough and true enough to "make good" in the terrible fight with the wilderness.

Nor was it only in that struggle to cut out their little homesteads from nature's stern forests that they had to toil, but also at the shaping of a nation in the love and practice of liberty and in the fear of God. As to the latter, many little old churches, dotted through the land, bear witness to the zeal of the missionaries and the people of early days; and as to the former, the free schools through all the country, the colleges, the universities, the public libraries, the political system—with its merits and defects—are in large measure the result of the efforts of earlier generations.

Strange as it may appear, the most northern part of this vast province is no farther north than the central part of Scotland, and its most southerly point (the most southerly of the whole Dominion) is in about the latitude of Rome. It has no high mountains, though there is great diversity of surface, and the climate of the southerly and westerly portions of the peninsula of old Ontario is distinctly milder than that of Quebec or the prairie provinces. Of course there is great variety of temperature in different parts of this vast region. The lowlying districts bordering on the Great Lakes have, as might be expected, a more humid climate than places more inland and of greater altitude, but the winter of Ottawa resembles that of Montreal, and of course the cold is severe in the far north. It is, however, a fact that Canadians staying during the winter in England appear to feel the cold there more than English people do in the settled parts of Canada. Often, indeed, newly-arrived English people think that the dwellings of Canadians are kept too hot during the winter months; and perhaps they are. The practice of keeping the houses warm has some advantages, however. A somewhat severe "snap" of cold weather rarely works the havoc with the water-pipes in Canada that so frequently occurs during exceptionally cold weather in England; and people are able to use every room of their well-warmed habitations in a fashion which is of great advantage when the said houses are pretty fully occupied.

In a typical summer there is much sunshine and a good deal of hot weather; and then Canadians live much out of doors. Those of the dwellers in the cities who can afford to do so, often move early in the warm months to cottages beside some of the numerous lakes, and remain there throughout the summer. These cottages are generally more like wooden tents than houses, admitting the fresh air very freely. The country people also live much out of doors, but both men and women on the farms are too busy to take holidays during the hot season.

Besides her two boundary rivers, the Ottawa and the St. Lawrence, Ontario, which is a well-watered province, has many another fine stream; but perhaps the most striking of its natural features are its lakes, large and small. Passing up the St. Lawrence and skirting the provincial boundaries with one's face turned towards the west, one comes first to Lake Ontario; then turning south along the Niagara River (perhaps its famous "Falls" are what most untravelled Britons would think of first of any place in Canada), one reaches Lake Erie, passes north through the St. Clair lake and river to Lake Huron, and from that by the wonderful locks at Sault Ste. Marie into Lake Superior, from the head of which inland sea it is only a few hours' journey to Winnipeg. The interesting part of this imaginary voyage is that by the help of a few short canals it may be taken in reality. So every year millions of bushels of grain come from the wheat fields of the West to Montreal; and in a short time, thanks to improvements now under way, ocean-going steamers from Liverpool will be able to make an uninterrupted journey to Fort William, which is by rail almost a thousand miles from Montreal.

But if Ontario touched on none of the "Five Great Lakes" instead of upon four, which lie between her territories and those of the United States, she would still be a land of lakes, in right of Lake Simcoe and the Muskoka lakes, Lake Nipissing, Lake Abitibi, huge Lake Nipigon, the thousand-isled Lake of the Woods, and hundreds of others. Many of these contain great quantities of fish, though, so far as the "Great Lakes" are concerned, the "fish stories" of the pioneers read now like idle tales; but still the commercial fisheries of the province bring in over $2,333,000 (£480,000), and give employment to several thousand men. In 1909 the catches of trout and white fish were the most important.

Nevertheless, in this province the fisheries are a very small industry compared to mining, lumbering, manufactures and agriculture. Some twenty thousand men find employment in mines. The mineral taking first rank in Ontario as a revenue-producer is silver, of which the production in 1911 amounted to nearly $16,000,000 (£3,280,000). Pig iron, natural gas, nickel and copper came next on the list.

The discovery of the rich silver deposits at Long's Lake, now Cobalt, was made by contractors engaged in building the Timiskaming and Northern Ontario Railway. About a month later—so the story goes—a blacksmith, La Rose, flung his hammer at an impudent fox. The missile struck a rock and made a bright metallic streak, which led to another great find. Not quite at once was the public persuaded of the value of these discoveries; then there was a mad rush to prospect for silver; and a town sprang up, looking, it is said, as if its makeshift houses had been "built between darkness and dawn." An Indian is credited with the finding of gold-bearing quartz on the shores of Larder lake.

Years earlier, in 1884, the vast deposits of nickel a few miles west of Sudbury were cut into by the construction of the Canadian Pacific Railway, but there the mineral which first attracted attention was copper. This was sent to be smelted in New Jersey, and it was only when experts detected the presence of nickel in the slag that the true value of the Sudbury mines was recognized.

The forests of Ontario are of vast importance, and promise to remain so. It is satisfactory to add that the state owns the forests, to a large extent, in Ontario (as in Quebec), and the expenses of the provincial government are met by the revenues from the Crown lands and the Dominion subsidy without the need of laying a cent of taxation upon the people. Of course, whether they realize it or not, the indirect taxes, which are collected by the Dominion government, come out of their pockets, and there are municipal taxes, the weight of which varies very much in different municipalities, being naturally much heavier in the cities than in the country.

But to return to the forests. Including about one hundred thousand square miles of woodlands in the new district of Patricia, which is only partially explored, the total forest area of Ontario is estimated at 202,000 square miles. Of this about twenty thousand square miles is under licence, and in 1912 the revenue from the forests amounted to considerably over $2,000,000 (£410,000), whilst the revenue so collected since Confederation amounts to about $44,000,000 (£9,040,000). This has been derived from ground rents, timber dues, transfer fees, and bonuses (that is, sums offered over and above the fixed charges for the right to cut timber). In 1911 the value of the timber cut in Ontario was nearly equal to that of the "cut" in all the rest of the Dominion.

An Act passed in 1898 empowered the government to set apart "Forest Reserves, to be owned in perpetuity by the Crown and operated for timber crops," and Ontario has now six forest reserves, which with Algonquin and Rondeau parks—chiefly intended for the preservation of game—amount in all to 20,000 square miles. The great northern forests consist largely of spruce, and there are half a dozen pulp and paper mills in operation in places easily accessible to these forests. Wood-pulp, by the way, is used in making car-wheels, coffins, pails, roofing materials and a long list of other articles. Ontario has still considerable forests of white and red pines, the trees, which were at one time counted by the lumbermen the only ones of value, being easily floated down to the sea, and being in great demand for masts and other uses. In Southern Ontario there used to be quantities of black walnut and other trees which would now be prized for making furniture, but in the days of the pioneers, owing to lack of transport facilities, vast piles of such woods were heaped together and burned.

In manufacturing, Ontario is the premier province, for though its capital comes in this respect second to Montreal, six Ontario cities are included amongst the first fourteen manufacturing centres of the Dominion. These are Toronto, Hamilton, Ottawa, London, Brantford, and Berlin; and in addition there are many smaller industrial centres. The industrial establishments (taken at random) include lumber and flour mills, agricultural implement works, shipbuilding yards, iron and steel plants, foundries, railway shops, distilleries, canning factories, cheese factories, creameries, carriage and motor car works. A long list of others might be added, and these various industries offer a variety of opportunity to skilled workmen.

But after all, Ontario is still chiefly an agricultural country; and the value of her field crops is "more than that of any other two provinces." In fact, the value of her whole agricultural products was estimated in 1911 at three hundred million dollars (about £60,000,000).

The province has a great variety of soils and climates, and its older parts are a region of "mixed farming"; where dairying, the raising of live stock; the growing of wheat, oats, and other grain; fruit culture, tobacco-growing, poultry-raising and bee-keeping are successfully carried on. Dairying, according to an official statement, "is the largest industry in the country"; and three-fourths of the dairy product of the whole Dominion is produced in Ontario.

1. TORONTO UNIVERSITY.

2. CANADIAN NORTHERN RAILWAY ELEVATOR AT PORT ARTHUR.

3. TORONTO: CORNER OF SPADINA AVENUE & QUEEN STREET, TORONTO.

The province produces also three-fourths of the fruit grown in Canada—chiefly in its southern counties bordering on the Great Lakes—and is almost equally famous for its apples and its peaches, its berries and its grapes. Hundreds of thousands of acres in Southern Ontario are planted with fruit trees and small fruit bushes; and immense areas of land equally suitable for fruit-culture remain to be planted—in the Niagara district, along the shores of Lakes Erie and Ontario, and in other districts.

From the point of view of opportunity for newcomers, the interesting feature of the situation is not what has been, but what may be done. The fact is, even in the older portions of the province, only the fringe of possible productivity has been touched, and here in Ontario we are still in the region where the country districts have suffered in the last few decades by the exodus of the young—at first largely to the United States, later to the West and to the cities. The result is that there are plenty of good farms for sale at prices ranging from $25 (£5) to $100 (£20) the acre—the latter price including the cost of buildings—and a list of these can be obtained from the "Director of Colonization" at Toronto.

The prices, by the way, of apple and peach orchards and of vineyards in good bearing go up far beyond the prices of ordinary farm lands. As much as from $400 (£80) to $1,200 (£240) an acre is asked in the Niagara district for peach orchards, according to age, while apple orchards may fetch from $300 (£60) to $500 (£100) an acre. Even unplanted lands good for fruit culture range high—$400 (£80) the acre being asked for land especially suitable for peach-growing.

There are many districts of Ontario where capable British farmers with some little capital would have every prospect of doing well, for markets for all produce are good. Conditions of life in the settled farming districts of this province are usually found pleasant by those who like a country life, and many things are working together to render these even better than they were a few years ago. I will, however, return to this matter a little later.

One of the great difficulties that Ontario farmers have to contend with is that of obtaining sufficiency of help in the busy seasons. The best remedy for this is to so manage the farm—by keeping a considerable number of live stock—that help can profitably be employed all the year round, and to have houses in which married men can live with their families.

This brings us naturally to the other side of the question—whether or not a good experienced farm man can get work. The wages given to a married man range from $250 (£50) to $350 (£70) the year, to which are added (as a rule) a rent-free cottage, and some extras such as milk and firewood. Often both the wife and children (as they grow out of early childhood) can also earn something. The wages for unmarried men of eighteen years of age and upwards, according to experience, or lack of it, range from $10 (£2) to $25 (£5) the month—in a few cases to $35 (£7)—with board, lodging and washing free. Board and lodging usually means living with the farmer's family, and there is no question that a man of good physique, good intelligence, real willingness to work and some thrift can soon attain a position of independence. As one newcomer to an Ontario farm expressed it, here "the boss hunts for a man, not the man for a job."

It is often wise for a newcomer to work for a while for someone else and to gain experience before attempting to acquire a farm for himself; but it must not be forgotten that, besides the numerous farms in well-settled districts that may be bought at prices which are often little more than yearly rents asked for land in England, there are Crown lands in Ontario, some of which are offered for sale at the nominal price of 50 cents (2*s.*) the acre—payable in four instalments with interest—and some which are given away free. But there are conditions attached to the sale or granting of Crown lands. In the first place, these lands can be acquired only by a male settler over eighteen, or the mother of a family who has residing with her at least one child under eighteen. The settler must live for three years on the homestead, and within this time must clear and cultivate about 10 per cent. of the land, and build a small habitable house. The size of the grant or farm lot is generally one hundred and sixty acres; and in the case of free grants there is usually a provision that an adjoining eighty to one hundred acres may be purchased at 50 cents per acre. Often, but not invariably, the Crown lands are sold subject to timber licences or to a reservation of minerals.

The public lands for sale are situated chiefly in Nipissing, Timiskaming, Sudbury, Algoma, and Rainy River districts; and those offered as free grants are in the districts of Nipissing, Timiskaming, Algoma, Kenora, Rainy River, and in the tract of land "lying between the Ottawa river and the Georgian bay, and comprising the northerly portions of the counties of Renfrew, Frontenac, Lennox and Addington, Hastings, Peterborough, Victoria and Simcoe; and the districts of Muskoka and Parry Sound."

Across Northern Ontario stretches the great fertile (so-called) "Clay Belt" of sixteen million acres, discovered during the surveys for the making of the Grand Trunk Pacific Railway; and this is within easy reach of the more settled parts of the province, viâ the town of North Bay, which is served by the Canadian Pacific Railway, the Grand Trunk, and the provincial government line, the Timiskaming and Northern Ontario Railway. The latter strikes in a north-westerly direction, two hundred and fifty miles, to Cochrane, where it joins the Grand Trunk Pacific, passing on the way through the Cobalt mining region. Altogether, Ontario has more than ten thousand miles of steam and electric railways, and this mileage is increasing very fast.

The Clay Belt is well wooded, but is not very difficult to clear, and the pioneers there, unlike their predecessors in old Ontario, find a ready sale for their wood. One man, after paying for the cutting of the timber on the sixteen acres of his purchase from government of one hundred and sixty acres, which he was bound to clear to obtain his title, sold the wood at a profit of $550 (£110), and this left him a balance of $90 (£18) after the cost of "stumping" and ploughing the land, which, as he put it, will "clear itself ready for crop." The timber is not always so valuable as this, but usually some money may be made from it. A couple of years later this same man stated that he had made a profit on his farm of nearly $1,200 (£240).

THE MOON CHUTE, NEAR BALA, ONTARIO.

There is also a chance for the settler to earn ready money by working on the roads which the government is making through the country, whilst the demands of the railway construction camps for farm produce insures a good market. It is only right to add, however, that *the beginner has to face inevitable hardships*, and though a strong, capable man may not only succeed, but enjoy the life, there are other men who might do well under different conditions, but prove failures as pioneers. At certain times of the year, black flies and mosquitoes are very troublesome, but this is a condition which will improve as the country becomes more settled.

In the study of ethnology, people are accustomed to speak of the stone age, the bronze age, and so forth; and in the study of social conditions in this province one might use the dwellings of the people as a criterion. But, while thousands of families are still in the "log-cabin" age, with all the concomitant disadvantages of roughness and loneliness, more have passed into the age of "frame houses"—which may be models of neatness and comfort, and are often the scenes of pleasant sociabilities—a smaller number are in the brick age—typical of urban conveniences and (ofttimes) conventionalities; and a very few have arrived even at the dignity of the "stone age," which from this point of view stands for wealth and luxury.

The population of Ontario is chiefly of British origin. Within the province are two capital cities—Ottawa, seat of the Dominion government, and Toronto, of the Provincial government. The local House has but one chamber, elected, it is commonly said, "by the people," but actually by the adult males of the population.

There is no state church, but all the leading denominations, and many smaller ones, are represented. The University of Toronto (which has more than four thousand undergraduates) is non-sectarian, but there are a number of other universities and colleges connected with the several churches. The education of children is free, and their attendance at school compulsory. The school system begins with the kindergarten, and leads up through the public school and the high school to the university. There are unsectarian public schools and Roman Catholic "separate" schools.

Amongst other valuable educational agencies in the province there were in 1912 four hundred and seventeen public and two hundred and forty-two travelling libraries, which reach many a remote village and lumber camp, and three hundred and seventy-five agricultural and eighty horticultural societies. In this connection it may be mentioned that the Ontario Agricultural College and Experimental Farm at Guelph enrolled, in 1911, no less than 1,500 students, whilst the Farmers' Institutes and Women's Institutes number their members by thousands. There are, of course, numerous associations and societies in the cities and towns for the furtherance of objects of a religious, philanthropic, or educational character, but the comparatively recent increase of associations of farmers and farmers' wives and daughters is especially interesting, because the enriching and development of rural social life touches a problem of national importance. These associations may prove of much advantage to the newcomer willing to profit by them.

According to the last census, considerably over half the population of Ontario is urban, but in the settled districts at least such recent innovations as rural telephones and mail deliveries are making the country life easier and more attractive. Men, accustomed to farm labour in the "Old Country," seem to be astonished at the number of labour-saving machines employed on the farms, and, in some localities, farmers share in the advantages of the "Hydro-Electric Power," developed from Niagara under the management of a government commission.

But, after all, it is not only material good things for which the emigrant seeks when he leaves his home-land. I have said something of the schools already, I might have said more of the churches which everywhere—in the crowded cities, in the quiet country, and in the lonely wilderness, sometimes nobly, sometimes feebly—are doing work for the growing nation which only they can do. I might tell of the vigorous, and upon the whole, successful, struggle which men and women are making in the cause of temperance—in Ontario and in other provinces—and of other efforts, needed even in this new land of opportunities, to prevent the exploiting of helpless children and young girls by greedy money-makers, to stamp out tuberculosis, to guard infant life, to cleanse the land of evils, physical and spiritual.

Ontario—and the Dominion—is, indeed, a land of endeavour as well as of opportunity, but the people are not too busy to find time to be helpful, and amongst the abiding impressions left from the years spent by the writer as an inexperienced worker on an Ontario farm, is that of the kindness and friendliness of neighbours, some of whom remembered similar experiences. And the hard work of the life was lightened by the loveliness of a beautiful country, and by no little pleasant sociability.

XI

MANITOBA, OLD AND NEW

THOUGH it had an area larger than that of Ireland, Scotland and Wales combined, Manitoba for many years suffered under a sense of injustice with regard to its restricted size. People called it "the postage-stamp province," but in 1912 that reproach was taken away by the addition to it of a "new Manitoba," more than twice the size of the old. Now the enlarged province boasts itself as "the Maritime Prairie Province," for it stretches away eastward to the shores of Hudson Bay, which was the old-time gateway of the seafaring British into the great West.

The Manitoba coast has two good natural harbours, Fort Churchill and Port Nelson, which, while they are by rail nine or ten hundred miles nearer to Winnipeg than is Montreal, are only about the same distance as the St. Lawrence port from Liverpool. What this may mean in the future to Manitoba can at present only be guessed at, but there seems little doubt that suitably-built steamships will be able to navigate Hudson Bay and Strait for a longer period annually than was the case with the little sailing vessels of the Hudson Bay Company, which were sometimes becalmed, as well as checked by quantities of ice.

But of more importance to prospective immigrants than the possibilities of the new-old waterway to Manitoba is the climate of the province itself. Now one must admit frankly that Manitoba has a cold winter, but it is not usually a very long one. Often the fine weather lasts late into the autumn, and seeding generally begins in April. Moreover, owing to the dryness of the atmosphere and the amount of sunshine, people do not suffer from the cold as the readings of the thermometer might lead the inexperienced to expect. It is a country where, both for health and comfort, it is necessary in winter to keep the houses warm and to wear good warm clothing out of doors, but ordinarily healthy people, who know how to take proper precautions, do not appear to dread the cold. It is, however, very hard on the poor, though more fortunate persons find the crisp cold exhilarating, and the climate is generally regarded as healthy. In summer the days are often hot, but the nights are usually cool and pleasant for sleeping, though there are seasons when flies and mosquitoes, at least in little-settled districts, are very troublesome.

The climate is unquestionably favourable for the growth of wheat and many other agricultural products. Despite the remarkable dryness and clearness of the atmosphere, Manitoba is not a dry and thirsty land where no water is, and in June there is usually ample rainfall after seeding to give the young crops every chance of growth. The frost coming out of the ground in spring, and the rains, have indeed a deplorable effect on the prairie trails. Not very long ago the streets of Winnipeg were sometimes almost impassable with mud, but Winnipeg—according to a table recently compiled by the meteorological department in Toronto—has a much greater annual rainfall than most other places in the province.

Manitoba has numerous and large lakes. Among those in the older part of the province are Winnipeg, Manitoba, Winnipegosis and Dauphin lakes, all very large according to old-world standards, and its chief rivers are the Red, Assiniboine, Winnipeg and Pembina, each with several tributaries. The waters of all these find their way ultimately into Hudson Bay.

Manitoba is popularly supposed to be "as flat as a pancake," and the prairie about Winnipeg is extraordinarily level in appearance. But, as a matter of fact, the prairie country of the Canadian West consists of three distinct steppes. Of these, Manitoba contains the whole of the first, and a portion of the second steppe. The first slopes gently from the international boundary, where it is about fifty miles wide, towards the far-distant Arctic Ocean, and the site of Winnipeg is only about seven hundred feet above sea-level, but the average elevation of the second steppe, which begins in South-west Manitoba, is about sixteen hundred feet. The face of this second steppe forms the "Riding and Duck Mountains," and the Porcupine hills, in which is the highest point in Manitoba, 2,500 feet. In the south there are two other elevations named, like many another natural feature of the prairie regions, after birds, fish or animals. These are the Turtle and the Tiger hills.

There are also acres of forest land in the north-west and extreme east of the old province, and here and there are small timbered districts, which supply the settlers with a certain amount of house timber and fuel, though not a little has to be imported. Much of new Manitoba is covered with forests, and is likely to supply immense quantities of pulpwood, and timber for other purposes. It is believed also to contain great stretches of good agricultural land; there are hopeful indications of mineral wealth; and its fisheries must be valuable. Finally, this wild north land certainly contains abundance of water power, which in time may make it an important manufacturing region. As yet the worth of its scarcely explored resources cannot be estimated, but quite enough is known to justify the Manitobans in congratulating themselves on the possession of this vast addition to the province.

But, leaving new Manitoba out of account, there is no lack of definite information concerning the older portion of this first-settled of the "Prairie Provinces." If one goes back to explorers and fur traders, its history may be said to begin far back in the eighteenth century with the building of La Verendrye's little trading post on the site of the modern city of Winnipeg. If we do not care to go behind the first attempt actually to colonize what is now Manitoba, the story stretches just over one hundred years.

It was in 1811 that Lord Selkirk obtained a large tract of land on the Red river from the Hudson Bay Company (of which he was a member), with the view of settling upon it an agricultural colony. The first party of British immigrants—drawn chiefly from Scotland—came in, it will be noted, by way of Hudson Bay, a route which it is prophesied may yet be preferred by British colonists as the shortest road to the great West. But no Hudson Bay Railroad was dreamed of when those first immigrants arrived, late in 1811, and it was not till the following summer that they reached their destination on the Red river.

LOOKING DOWN MAIN STREET, WINNIPEG.

There they received anything but a hospitable welcome. In fact, the Hudson Bay Company's rivals in the fur trade deliberately set themselves to make the place too hot to hold them, for, not altogether unreasonably, they regarded farming and fur trading as mutually exclusive industries. But neither their ill-will, which at last culminated in bloodshed, nor other disasters of various descriptions, sufficed to destroy the colony. Through all, a few of Selkirk's settlers succeeded in the end in making good their footing; and many modern Manitobans are proud to claim descent from these sturdy and steadfast folk who, with no better implements than hoes, broke up the ancient sod, and sowed and reaped the first of Manitoba's famous wheat crops.

A few years later the rival trading companies amalgamated; but for the next half-century the growth of the colony—still under the rule of the Hudson Bay Company—was extraordinarily slow. Then it was affected by events in the eastern provinces.

Immediately after Confederation, resolutions were passed in the Canadian parliament asking the British Government to add to the Dominion these great regions in the north and west, and in 1869 the Hudson Bay Company consented to give up its trade monopoly and sovereign rights in consideration of a sum of £300,000 in money, and of about a twentieth part of the land yet to be surveyed south of the north branch of the Saskatchewan river and west of Lake Winnipeg.

In the Red River region there was at this time a population of about twelve thousand (chiefly half-breeds, and more of French than of English extraction). No one thought it necessary to consult them about the transfer, and when surveyors were sent into the country, the Red River farmers began to fear that their claims to their farms and their right to cut hay on the adjacent wild lands (a privilege of great value in their eyes) would be disregarded. Louis Riel, a young man who had been educated at Montreal, giving voice to their vague alarm, stirred them up to violent agitation, and soon the half-breeds were in open rebellion. They seized the Hudson Bay Company's post of Fort Garry (where Winnipeg now is) and set up a "Provisional Government," with Riel at its head. Some who dared to oppose his authority were imprisoned, and finally a young Irishman from Ontario Thomas Scott—after a mock trial, was brutally murdered. This roused a storm of indignation throughout Canada, and a body of regular troops and militiamen, under the command of Colonel (afterwards Lord) Wolseley, was sent to put down the insurrection. The journey from the east was so toilsome and difficult that, though the troops left Toronto in June, 1870, they did not reach the Red river till August; but Riel fled on their approach, and many of the militiamen who spent the winter in Manitoba ultimately settled there.

In the same year the government of the country as a Canadian province was inaugurated. Manitoba followed Ontario in having only a single chamber in the Provincial Legislature; and it is represented in the Dominion parliament by four members in the Upper, and ten in the Lower, House. "The electoral franchise is practically based on residence and manhood suffrage."

Between the taking of the first Dominion census affecting Manitoba in 1871, and the fourth (and last) the population of the province has been multiplied by eighteen, being set down in 1911 at 455,614; but, while the urban population showed an increase in the previous decade of nearly one hundred and thirty thousand, the rural population increased only by a little over seventy thousand five hundred.

The growth of Winnipeg during these forty years has been extraordinary. In 1871 it was a mere village of two hundred and thirteen inhabitants. In 1912, owing largely to immigration from other lands, it was a city of well over two hundred thousand people. Its situation at the confluence of the Red and Assiniboine rivers was "strategic" in the days when canoes and bateaux were the commonest means of transport, but it was the building of the Canadian Pacific Railway which gave the first strong impetus to its growth; and now it is a great knot in a network of railway lines radiating in about thirty different directions. It is a growing industrial centre, with water power available in large quantity, and it employs over fifteen thousand workers in its factories, which include plants turning out structural steel; making traction engines for farmers; and occupied with food products. But still to-day it is the railways (Manitoba, by the way, now has over four thousand miles of railways) which give its chief importance to Winnipeg. It is the western headquarters of the three greatest Canadian railway systems, the Canadian Pacific, the Canadian Northern, and the Grand Trunk Pacific. Through it pours annually the vast stream of wheat from the grain fields of the West, for it is "the greatest grain market of the world"; whilst another stream flows westward—of more interest and account than any merchandize—the stream of humanity bound to the land of new chances. But part of this human river, as everywhere, tends to drift into the eddies. Some newcomers (foreigners and British alike) never get beyond Winnipeg, and some, failing on the land, return thither, rendering its social problems inexpressibly difficult.

For the past five years the Winnipeg Industrial Bureau has been diligently endeavouring to increase the industrial importance of the city by advertising its opportunities, giving information to persons thinking of engaging in manufacturing, opening a permanent exhibition of articles manufactured in the city and district, and encouraging technical education. Moreover, and this will be of special interest to some immigrants, it has a department to assist in bringing out the wives and children of British workmen who settle in Winnipeg. In little more than two years 1,591 persons have been assisted. In 1912 "234 wives, 215 children over twelve years of age and 465 children under twelve years of age" were brought out, and "of the families reunited 79 came to Winnipeg from Scotland, 165 from England and 14 from Ireland." A most satisfactory feature of the movement has been the way it has spread to other places; and within two years "Imperial Home Reunion Associations" were organized in Ottawa, in Montreal, Toronto, Edmonton, Halifax, and twenty other leading towns of the Dominion.

The people of Winnipeg believe in municipal ownership, and the city owns and operates waterworks, a street lighting system, a stone quarry, an asphalt plant and a hydro-electric light and power plant, which has reduced the cost of domestic lighting to less than one-third that formerly charged by a private company. Winnipeg is, moreover, a city of broad fine streets, and of numerous churches, schools and colleges. It is the seat of the University of Manitoba, which has six colleges, and of the Provincial Agricultural College, which was first opened in 1906. This college confers the degree of "Bachelor of Science in Agriculture" on those who successfully pass through its five winters' course. There is also a course of Home Economics for women, and in both cases the cost is very low compared to the high rates of living and of wages in the West. In connection with the college, "demonstration and instruction trains," with a special staff of lecturers and experts, are sent out over "practically every line in the province," to carry some of its benefits to the numbers of men and women who cannot attend the college. Of other efforts to aid and improve agriculture I have no space to write.

As to the education of the children, Winnipeg is a city of schools, and in the remotest settlements a school district may be formed as soon as there are ten children of school age (that is, from five to fifteen) in a section, and the schools are supported by grants from the provincial government, and by taxes levied on the people by their municipal councils. In 1905 the experiment of consolidated schools was first tried in Manitoba, and now there are a number of such schools, the children being carried to and from them in well-covered vans.

The growth of Winnipeg and other towns is no doubt largely connected with the growth of manufactures, which, according to official figures, has been phenomenally rapid since the beginning of this century. During its first decade, in fact, the value of manufactures in Manitoba increased by over 315 per cent. At present little mining is carried on, and though in 1910-11 the fisheries of the province brought in about one and one-third million dollars (£260,000), this is considerably less than the amount received by the farmers for the article of butter alone, and agriculture is emphatically the outstanding industry of Manitoba.

"Manitoba No. 1 Hard" wheat is famous throughout the world. Manitoba farmers, however, are discovering many other avenues to comfort and success than the almost exclusive growth of this grain, with the advantage of much better prospects to their lands of continued productivity than by the repetition, year after year, of a single crop. Still the province raises immense quantities of wheat, but mixed farming has its advocates, who not only preach but practise their favourite agricultural doctrine.

Nor is this wonderful, in a community which lives chiefly by agriculture and yet cannot begin to supply its own cities (nay, its own farmhouses!) with eggs and meat and dairy products. Last year, says a recent government publication, no less than $102,000 (£20,400) worth of milk and sweet cream was imported from the State of Minnesota for consumption in Winnipeg. At the same time, Winnipeg bought from Eastern Canada 1,700,000 pounds of creamery butter, chiefly for local distribution, and, besides, far-away New Zealand supplied some butter for the tables of Manitoba folk. As for eggs, three hundred thousand dozen, or twenty-five car-loads, were imported from the United States for Winnipeg, and smaller centres also bring them in by the car-load. Nor was this all. Cheese and poultry, sheep by the thousand, and bacon, hams and lard by car-loads, come from east and west and south to feed the people of the prairies.

AMONG THE WHEATFIELDS OF MANITOBA.

The point of all this is that these things might be supplied with profit to the farmer and advantage to the consumer from Manitoba's own land. There is no question about the demand for dairy produce, poultry, meat, vegetables and fruit. Neither is there any question that people, who know how, can produce these things in quantities within the province; and here is where one excellent opportunity for immigrants who understand something of gardening, dairying and poultry-raising comes in. Manitoba has excellent markets, good land, but she wants gardeners and farmers—especially farmers who will give attention to something besides wheat.

As for the land, only about one-sixth of the cultivable area in the older portion of the province is yet under cultivation; and the newcomer may either buy an improved farm (at prices ranging, according to soil, locality, etc., from $15 to $35, $40, or even $80 the acre (£3 to £16)), acquire school lands by purchase from the government (in which case there are no settlement conditions), or make entry for a homestead. In many municipalities—especially in the south of the province—all the homesteads have been taken up, but there still remain free homesteads available within one hundred and twenty-five miles of Winnipeg, with government and school lands at from $3 to $6 the acre (12*s.* to 24*s.*). (For conditions as to the homesteading or purchase of government lands, see Appendix, Note B, page 160.)

The Canadian Pacific Railway also has lands for sale in Manitoba.

The change which is gradually, but slowly, taking place from grain-growing exclusively to mixed farming is resulting in the breaking up of the very large farms, and this will greatly improve social conditions; enabling neighbours to be more neighbourly, strengthening the scattered congregations of the churches, and making life brighter for young and old alike.

Of the population, a considerable proportion are natives of Canada—some of these speaking French—or of the British Isles. There are, too, a number of people who have come from the United States. Nearly one-fifth are foreigners in origin; but the younger members of the alien races soon learn to speak English, and to adopt Canadian ways. By the way, the famous "No. 1 Hard" Manitoba wheat is said to have been grown first by a colony of Mennonites from Ontario, who settled south of Winnipeg. The word is not the name of a race, but of a religious sect, and, according to the latest census returns, of its forty-four or forty-five thousand representatives in Canada, Manitoba can claim over one-third.

The strongest of any religious denomination is the Presbyterian, with the Anglican second, the Roman Catholic third, and the Methodist fourth; but forty or fifty other "religions" are represented in the province (which is, indeed, not peculiar in this respect) by groups of adherents counting, like the Lutherans and the Greek-Catholics, by thousands, or like the Deists and Mohammedans, by twos and threes.

There is a great demand for workers in the busy season on the farms. Farm labourers, during the summer, may expect from $25 (£5) to $40 (£8) a month, and, during winter, from $5 (£1) to $20 (£4), in both cases with board. In harvest time skilled men may receive as much as $50 (£10) the month, or $2 to $3 (8*s.* to 12*s.*) the day, subject to deduction if bad weather prevents work. Ordinary labourers get $2 or $8 (8*s.* to 12*s.*) a day without board, and lumbermen in the camps $30 (£6) the month, with board and lodging.

Often there is also a good demand for skilled industrial workers, but this varies greatly from time to time; and it is *most important* that before setting out the intending immigrant should obtain *recent information* concerning the industrial conditions in the locality where he thinks of settling. For addresses of persons who will give information, see Appendix A, pp. 159-160.

Carpenters in Winnipeg get 35 cents to 40 cents (1*s.* 5*d.* to 1*s.* 8*d.*) the hour. Bricklayers and masons receive about 67½ cents (2*s.* 9*d.*) the hour, but cannot work at their trade for more than seven or eight months in the year. Tailors get $17 the week, and printers $18 to $20 the week. In considering these high wages (amounting to £3 or £4 the week), it must be remembered that house rent, food, and the cost of fuel are also very high; but, in spite of all such disadvantages, the fact remains that for the young, strong, thrifty worker, Manitoba has great opportunities.

XII

SASKATCHEWAN, THE WHEAT PROVINCE

TO borrow a threadbare but expressive phrase, "Wheat is king," in Saskatchewan. Go where one will, in the inhabited part of the province, one is never allowed to forget this. One travels through miles on miles of wheat fields, and the most conspicuous building at many a wayside station is a giant "elevator"—if there does not chance, indeed, to be a row of these. Every budding town seems to begin with an agricultural implement "depot"; and near the railway stations in the cities self-binders, gasoline engines, and threshing machines, gaudy with yellow and crimson paint, are drawn up, awaiting their purchasers, by the hundred.

Nor is this the only token of the empire of King Wheat! In train and city, as well as at the tables of the farmers, the talk is of weather—good or bad—for the sowing and the harvest, for in Saskatchewan every man, woman and child realizes that in the last analysis the dependence of the whole community is on the measure of success which attends the cultivation of the soil. Wheat is king; and as in the old days every road led to Rome, so in writing of Saskatchewan—though this is true to a certain extent of most of the Canadian provinces—it is impossible to avoid coming back again and again to the farmer and his crops and his doings, his difficulties and his successes, and his way of meeting all kinds of problems. Here at least he is the hero of the drama—the central figure in the picture, and therefore I shall make no apology for seeming to travel in a circle.

Let us speak first of the kingdom of wheat.

Saskatchewan, in the south, has a breadth of three hundred and ninety miles, and a length of about seven hundred and fifty miles, or an area of somewhat over a quarter of a million square miles, including a water surface of about eight thousand three hundred miles, made up chiefly of lakes, large and small. It is larger than France, and over twice the size of the British Isles, with which it roughly corresponds in latitude. Edinburgh, by the way, is further north than any part of Saskatchewan yet settled, and the northern boundary of the province—the 60th parallel of north latitude—touches the two European capitals, Christiania of Norway and St. Petersburg of Russia.

It comprises the greater part of "the second prairie steppe," which has an average elevation of about fifteen hundred feet above sea-level, but Lake Athabasca, thrusting itself into its extreme north-west, is less than seven hundred feet above the sea, and the highest summit of the Cypress hills is over four thousand two hundred feet. Thus this "prairie province" is by no means all a level plain. In fact, it possesses such differences of surface that it has been said that it may be divided into "four well-defined zones." In the south (with the exception of some hilly districts) and extending to Saskatoon is the rolling prairie. Next comes a belt of mingled prairie and woodlands, dotted with small lakes, and often described as park-like. Then, about Prince Albert, begins the great northern forest of "spruce, tamarac, jack-pine, poplar and birch." This timbered belt crosses the province, and is between three and four hundred miles wide. North of it is the fourth zone, only sparsely wooded.

The province is situated in the very heart of the Dominion, but it is watered by several great rivers, which have cut their way deep into the plains. One of these, the Saskatchewan or "Rushing Water," as the Indians called it—has given its name to the province in which its two branches, the North and the South Saskatchewan, unite to flow together into Lake Winnipeg and thence to Hudson Bay. Farther north the mightiest river is the Churchill, one thousand miles long, which by many a tumultuous rapid hurries to the same inland sea.

For a long time Saskatchewan had a bad reputation so far as climate is concerned, and if any British immigrant comes to settle in the country without understanding that the winters are very much colder than those he has been accustomed to, he will probably be much disappointed and may feel himself ill-used, though the chances are that he ought to have made more particular inquiries before he came. The disadvantages of the climate are a low winter temperature (for ten years the *average* temperature of the coldest months, January and February, shows from 27 to 29 degrees of frost); an occasional severe snowstorm or "blizzard," and some dry windy weather at other seasons of the year, when the blowing of the dust is very trying.

The advantages, often held by residents in Saskatchewan of more than two or three years' standing to outweigh the disadvantages, are the clear exhilarating atmosphere, the light snowfall, the bright sunshine at all seasons, the cool, pleasant nights of summer, and the infrequence of rain or thaws during winter. Usually the cold weather does not reach its greatest severity till after Christmas, and winter may be said to end late in March. The sowing of the crops occasionally begins in March, but generally not until April.

It used to be supposed that the climate of the province was too severe to allow grain crops to come to perfection, but a few years ago the experiment of growing wheat was made successfully a little east of Regina, at Indian Head (where, by the way, are situated a Dominion experimental farm and forest nursery), and in 1911, at the "Land Exhibition" in New York, a prize of $1,000 (£205) in gold, offered by Sir Thomas Shaughnessy for the best "one hundred pounds of milling wheat grown in America," was carried off by a sample of Marquis wheat, grown on a farm near Rosthern, about forty miles north of Saskatoon. The Marquis variety of wheat was originated by the "Dominion cerealist," Dr. Charles Saunders, on the Central Experimental Farm at Ottawa, and the prize sample was grown by Mr. Seager Wheeler, an Englishman from the Isle of Wight who had been farming in Saskatchewan for fifteen years.

1. CUTTING WHEAT ON A 4,000 ACRE FARM NEAR SASKATOON, SASKATCHEWAN.

2. HASTINGS STREET, VANCOUVER, BRITISH COLUMBIA.

The importance of Saskatchewan as a wheat-growing region is only of recent development. When white men first settled in the country, a generation ago, they began with cattle ranching; now it is the prime wheat-growing province in the Dominion. In 1913 the crop amounted to 108,288,000 bushels; but though for years to come the actual yield of this grain is likely to increase enormously, for the land at present under crop does not, it is said, greatly exceed that set apart for roads, there are signs that in the future other products of the farm will dispute the almost exclusive sway of King Wheat. For example, at the International Exhibition at Lethbridge, in 1912, Saskatchewan won the first prize for the "best collection of farm products." One argument in favour of changing to a greater diversity of crops is that it tends to simplify the labour problem, as the harvesting of different crops is spread over a longer period than that of wheat alone.

At present about 80 per cent. of the population of the province belongs to the farming class, but the opportunities in Saskatchewan are not limited to the cultivation of the soil. The northern half of the province, lacking railways, is not yet ready for ordinary settlers, but in the great woods north of Prince Albert the lumber industry is important. In fact, in 1911, between eight and nine thousand men found employment in the lumber camps and mills. There is, by the way, a vast demand in the West for railway ties or "sleepers," and this is largely supplied by the jack-pine of the northern woods.

Flouring mills, as might be expected, are amongst the chief of Saskatchewan's industrial establishments, and brick-making plants are numerous. There is an excellent home market for bricks, and suitable clay is found in every quarter, north, south, east and west. There are already several companies making structural steel for bridges, and soon large iron works will be established at Prince Albert, deposits of good iron ore having been discovered in the northern wilderness.

Prince Albert (of which the first house is said to have been the log-cabin of a Presbyterian missionary, put up in 1866) is rich in the so-called "white coal," and before long the city will be supplied with hydro-electric power from the La Colle falls in the Saskatchewan river, which flows past her very doors. The damming of the river to develop the power will serve the purpose of improving its navigability, and it is anticipated that soon there will be steamboat communication between Lake Winnipeg and Edmonton. In the south, just within the borders of the province, near Roche Percée, and away in a north-westerly direction along the eastern escarpment of the "third prairie steppe," lignite or "brown coal" has been found in many different places, and in Saskatchewan there were thirty mines in 1910, employing in all nearly four hundred persons.

It is difficult to exaggerate the part played in Saskatchewan by the railways. Lying almost midway between the Pacific and the communication by means of the Great Lakes and the St. Lawrence with the Atlantic, this region had no outlet for any of the products of its fertile soil till the coming of the railways. In truth, there were no products, but only possibilities, for the settlers came in after the Canadian Pacific Railway—the pioneer line—which crossed the province on its way to the far west; and since then branch lines and little new towns have grown up together, till now this one great railway has over two thousand four hundred miles of "steel" in Saskatchewan alone, and its single track of 1885 (which it was such a mighty feat to build through the lone prairies and across the rugged western mountains) has become a complicated network. But what this first line meant in binding the separated provinces into a real union was shown in that very year, 1885, when for the second time the half-breeds, led by Louis Riel, rose in revolt.

This time the storm centre was in the North-West Territories—from which in 1905 the new provinces of Saskatchewan and Alberta were carved out—far west and north of the Red River, but though there were long gaps in the railway, the troops sent from Eastern Canada reached the scene of the disturbance in about a month, or less than half the time which it had taken Wolseley's force to reach the Red River fifteen years earlier. During the last ten or twelve years a younger railway company, the Canadian Northern, which in 1901 had not a mile of line in operation in Saskatchewan, has been adding line to line, and branch to branch, entering new districts, where farmers had gone in on the promise of its coming, carrying into the country immigrants and "settlers' effects" by the car-load, and out of it train upon train of wheat. It also is knotting together a network across southern Saskatchewan. Last year its lines in the province had lengthened to 1,785 miles, and it is still reaching forward in many directions, including that of Hudson Bay.

Lastly, the luxurious passenger trains of the Grand Trunk Pacific are crossing Saskatchewan, with the promise of another easy ocean-to-ocean route; and the promise also of additional means of transportation for the annual millions of bushels of Saskatchewan's wheat. But more quickly even than the railway companies have been pushing the construction of their new lines increases the product of the fields and farms; and every new avenue of transportation, while improving the situation in certain districts, also adds to the magnitude of the problem to be solved, for there are always people, regardless of isolation and hardships, ready to go in advance of the railways.

At present the authorities are giving no encouragement to immigrants to settle in the northern part of Saskatchewan, for that district is entirely without transportation facilities, and is better suited to the wandering, adventurous lives of the hunter and trapper than of the would-be maker of a new home. The former serve best, perhaps, as heroes for boyish romances of the Ballantyne type; but the real interest of the story of the Canadian West belongs to the home-makers—the nation-builders—who are surging in to take possession of the land.

In 1901, the population of Saskatchewan was nearly 91,300; in 1911, it was over 492,400, when, by the way, the male population exceeded the female by 91,000. During 1911, 44,000 immigrants settled in Saskatchewan. Of these 59 per cent. were Americans, whose experience of farming under similar conditions makes them excellent settlers; whilst the remaining number, which entered by ocean ports, represented no less than forty-six nationalities. Amongst the homesteaders for the year, besides Canadians from the east, and people from the British Isles and from the United States, were French, Germans, Belgians and Hollanders, Swiss, Italians, Roumanians, Syrians, Austro-Hungarians, Russians, Danes and Icelanders, Swedes and Norwegians. The people from Northern Europe make particularly good settlers, and though some of the foreigners appear to be of an unpromising type as material for the building up of a nation on British lines, they are often found, on closer acquaintance, to have some special excellence to contribute to the general "melting pot." The assimilation of all these peoples is no small problem for the young Dominion, however.

In Saskatchewan, as elsewhere, perhaps the greatest force for the Canadianizing of the newcomers is the common school, which has an influence extending into the home circles of the children who attend. It is fortunate for the nation that a large proportion of the teachers (chiefly young women) hold a high view of their calling, and therefore are peculiarly well-suited to act as guides to the newcomers.

The different churches in the province are also toiling bravely amongst the immigrants, but their task is complicated by differences of race, language and traditions; and by the tendency of the population to scatter itself in little groups—sometimes only a single family and sometimes even one individual—far and wide, wherever fertile land is to be had. Of late years immigrants have been coming in so fast, that the churches, though adding constantly to their force of men and women, clergymen and missionaries have great difficulty in overtaking the work; in fact, they cannot do it.

In Saskatchewan the leading denomination is the Presbyterian; then follow the Roman Catholics, the Methodists, the Anglicans, the Lutherans, the Greek-Catholics, the Baptists and the Mennonites.

Despite all that is being done, many of the settlers are for years out of reach of church services, and some of the groups of foreigners are practically left to themselves in this respect, for want of people to work amongst them. For enforcing law and order amongst the scattered settlers and for many other services, Saskatchewan owes much to the small body of North-West Mounted Police, who have inculcated respect for British justice in the breasts of red and white men, newcomers and old settlers.

The Saskatchewan people themselves are wrestling valiantly with their own problems, religious, educational, social. In this connection it is interesting to note that a place in Saskatchewan—Sintaluta, near Indian Head—was the birthplace of that powerful organization of farmers, the "Grain-Growers' Association," and that its founder, Hon. W. R. Motherwell, himself a farmer and a graduate of the Ontario Agricultural College at Guelph, is now the provincial Minister of Agriculture. This organization, with which is affiliated the "Grain-Growers' Association of Manitoba" and the "United Farmers" of Alberta, has led in the struggle against the great corporations, which were too much for the individual farmer, for better transportation and elevator facilities. Later, an accessory association was established called the "Grain-Growers' Grain Company," to enable the organized farmers to market their grain on a basis of co-operation.

NEW PARLIAMENT HOUSE, REGINA, SASKATCHEWAN.

This principle is growing in favour in Saskatchewan, and it is hoped that by its aid the conditions of life amongst the farming community may be made so desirable as to check the trend of population to the towns. Saskatchewan has now a co-operative elevator company, a co-operative telephone system in the rural districts, connected with government-owned trunk lines and city services—which is perhaps as great an advantage from the social as from the business point of view—and co-operative creameries, and insurance of crops against damage by hail, assisted by government. Moreover, in the University of Saskatchewan, at Saskatoon, scientific instruction in agriculture is given a first place, and great efforts are made to extend the influence and usefulness of the university to every class and locality in the province.

With regard to education, a rural school district may be established in Saskatchewan where there are four persons resident who would be liable to assessment, and at least twelve children between the ages of five and sixteen years. No district may exceed twenty-five square miles in area, but in practice districts are rarely so large. The schools are supported in part by local rates, and in part by provincial grants. Teachers' salaries in rural districts vary from $50 (£10) to $65 (£13) the month, whilst board can usually be obtained at from $12 (£2 8*s*.) to $15 (£3) the month. During the five years ending with 1910, the number of school districts more than doubled, no less than one thousand three hundred new ones being organized. There are also high schools and collegiate institutes, scattered through the province, where young people can obtain more advanced instruction.

Though primarily an agricultural province, Saskatchewan is dotted with enterprising little villages and growing towns, and has four small but busy and fast-growing cities. First comes Regina, the capital, where annually gather the members of the single chamber of the Provincial Legislature; next comes Saskatoon, a railway centre and the seat of the university; then the older cities of Moose Jaw and Prince Albert. The population of the largest of these is somewhere in the neighbourhood of thirty thousand; but in the Canadian West just at present figures become ridiculously out-of-date even in a few months.

Still, Saskatchewan holds wide her doors for others to enter. She wants men—and women—for her farms and her young towns. She has Dominion lands to offer as homesteads (see Appendix, Note B, page 160), and wild or improved lands which may be bought from the railways and other companies at from $10 (£2 8*s*.) the acre up to $30 (£6) or $40 (£8), according to locality, etc. There are opportunities for business and professional men, but the demand is greatest for workers on the farms. If engaged by the year, average wages for a good man would be about $25 (£5) the month, with board; but if the engagement were only for eight months, the average might be from $25 (£5) to $40 (£8) the month; while for harvesting and threshing only, men receive from $35 (£7) to $50 (£10) the month, or $2 to $3 (8*s*. to 12*s*.) the day; and every year "Harvesters' Excursions" are run from the east.

There is often a good demand in the cities and towns in summer for unskilled labour; and in the lumber camps in the winter; and sometimes newcomers of the artizan and mechanics' class can readily obtain work at their trades; but the demand fluctuates, and it is wise for such immigrants to take care to procure *reliable and recent* information before going to any town.

1. JASPER AVENUE, EDMONTON, ALBERTA.
2. STOOKING WHEAT, BENITA, SASKATCHEWAN.

Capable domestic servants are always in demand at wages of about $15 (£3) a month, and upwards. Anyone wishing for recent and particular information concerning the rates of wages, and the demand for workers in any special trade, could not do better, however, than write to the Secretary of the Bureau of Labour, Regina, Saskatchewan.

XIII

ALBERTA: WHERE PRAIRIES AND MOUNTAINS MEET

ALBERTA is in the same latitude as its sister province of Saskatchewan, is almost of the same size (being about three thousand square miles larger), and "came of age," as it were, or attained the rights of a province, upon the same day, September 1, 1905. Its situation, as an inland province very far from the eastern seaboard, and shut in from the west by mighty chains of mountains, has delayed its progress; but it has grown with the building of railways, and recently its population has shown the most rapid increase of any of the provinces. In the decade between the census years, 1901 and 1911, its increase was 424 per cent., and last year its population was swelled by about ninety thousand new arrivals, from the eastern provinces, the United States, and countries beyond the seas, including a goodly number of British.

It is a land of great natural wealth and wonderful variety of beauty, for within it the last elevated "prairie steppe" gives way to mountains with peaks that soar into the blue high above the snowline. The Rockies, indeed, form the irregular boundary line of the south-west, which divides Alberta from British Columbia; and there is many a noble mountain within the province, though one is often misled, by the inadequacies of the ordinary maps, into thinking of it almost wholly as a prairie land.

In the south the country is of the rolling prairie type, though its altitude is high; but further north it has the park-like character of woodlands, interspersed with open prairie, and further north still, though the park-like country still prevails in certain districts, the land in general is a forest-covered wilderness, broken by lakes and muskegs. The latter make summer journeys extremely difficult, and it is easier for the Indians and traders and missionaries, who at present are the sole inhabitants, to travel when winter has sealed up the lakes and morasses with ice, thus making possible short-cuts between places which in summer can be reached only by devious journeys up one stream and down another, with laborious portages between.

Edmonton is still a centre of the fur-trade, and even now, in winter time, picturesque dog-trains arrive from the north in the provincial capital, whilst in the heart of Alberta traders, surveyors, mail-carriers and missionaries are leading the kind of life described in the "Wild West" books of our childhood. Still, on winter's nights, in the white Albertan wilderness, many a man, for one motive or another, is sleeping out under the stars, defiant of the frost and loneliness; and still, in the long days of the northern summer, canoes ply on the rivers, which are the only roads in portions of Alberta.

Of the numerous lakes of the province, Athabasca, which Alberta shares with Saskatchewan, has a surface of 2,850 square miles, but Lesser Slave Lake, the largest entirely within the province, is only four hundred and eighty square miles in extent. The rivers of Alberta are more important than the lakes. The four principal are the North and the South Saskatchewan; the Athabasca and the Peace river, which all rise in the Rocky Mountains, flow in an easterly or north-easterly direction, and have numerous tributaries, amongst which are some which might themselves take rank as important rivers. Both lakes and rivers, by the way, abound in fish, white fish being a staple food of the Indians and of the few white men in the north, as well as of the dogs used as draught animals.

The climate resembles that of Saskatchewan in its cold winters, hot summer days, and its dry, bright weather all the year round. Sometimes the mercury sinks in winter far below zero; sometimes in summer it registers as high as 90 degrees in the shade; but the nights are never unbearably hot, and the weather is never of the "muggy" type which in some places makes exertion so distasteful. There is little difference between the mean summer temperature in various parts of the province, owing, perhaps, to the fact that the general altitude is much greater in the south than the north. As it approaches the mountains at the boundary, the country is about four thousand feet above sea-level, but it slopes gently downward towards the north and east, till in the far north the altitude is less than one thousand feet. The Peace River valley has as warm a summer as the valley of the Saskatchewan, three hundred miles to the south, and everywhere there are long hours of sunshine in the growing season.

The climate of parts of the province, even as far north as the Peace River valley, is much modified by the "chinook," winds which, tempered by the warm Japanese current of the North Pacific, blow through the passes of the Rocky Mountains, and sometimes even in mid-winter cause a rise of temperature of fifty or sixty degrees in a few hours. One effect of this is the melting of the snow with marvellous rapidity, and in an ordinary season horses and cattle can live and thrive on the open ranges all winter, though provident farmers keep a good supply of hay on hand for emergencies. In most parts of the province there is a sufficient rainfall for the needs of the crops, and the rain comes as a rule most abundantly when most needed, but there are districts in the south where irrigation is being practised with great success and advantage.

The natural resources of Alberta are varied and abundant. First and foremost is the soil, of which a well-known English agriculturist and chemist, Professor Farmer, wrote: "Although we have hitherto considered the black earth of central Russia the richest in the world, that land has now to yield its distinguished position to the rich, deep, black soil of Western Canada." Other experts bear almost equally strong testimony to the value of the soil of these provinces, but in Alberta it was estimated very recently that only about 3 per cent. of her hundred million acres suitable for farming is as yet cultivated.

1. MAKING A STREET, PRINCE RUPERT, BRITISH COLUMBIA.

2. MIRROR, ALBERTA—A PRAIRIE TOWN IN ITS FIRST SUMMER.

3. A SCHOOL HOUSE IN PRINCE RUPERT.

Farming there began in the wild, free, un-English form of cattle-raising on ranches, so large that sixty to one hundred acres of pasturage was allowed for each animal, in herds in some cases numbering thousands. The natural conditions of food, water springs, and sufficient shelter were so good that little attention was needed or given, and two men were supposed to be able to manage fifteen hundred head of cattle. The ranches were bought by large companies, or (more often) leased from government, and every year thousands of beasts were sent to the markets of the eastern provinces or to those of England. A few large ranches remain still, chiefly in the neighbourhood of MacLeod.

But now the dashing, picturesque "cow-boys" are fast passing away. Their place is being taken by farmers of a more plodding type, and every year sees more railway lines cutting into the old-time ranches, and more homesteaders arriving to build their little shacks and villages in the lands which were once the pasture ground of innumerable buffaloes, and then of cattle scarcely less wild.

There are, however, a multitude of farmers who continue on a small scale the stock-raising industry, and in 1910 there were actually twice as many head of cattle in Alberta as there were in 1901, though there were still not quite as many as there had been in 1906. The fact is that though grain-growing offers the line of least resistance for the establishment of many a newcomer, who has not the means to purchase stock, and is obliged to turn to something that will speedily bring a return in ready money, the belief in "mixed" as opposed to exclusive grain farming is gaining ground in Alberta, as elsewhere in Canada. Besides its other advantages it prevents the farmer suffering so severely in a bad year, when his risk is divided between different kinds of agricultural products.

It required some experiment to discover the class of wheat best adapted to Alberta's soil and climate; but in 1902 seed was imported from Kansas of the variety known as "Turkey Red," and it so improved in the new region that it soon won wider fame than before under the new name of "Alberta Red."

This is a winter wheat, and the plan is favoured in this province of sowing both spring and winter wheat, as it spreads out the labour of sowing and harvesting into two periods instead of one. Winter wheat grows best in the southern district, but, though not quite so hard when grown further north, where the rainfall is greater, "Alberta Red" still proves an excellent crop in many parts of the province, and year by year a large additional acreage is sown with it. Other grain crops usually give a very satisfactory result, though, of course, the yield is much affected by weather conditions.

Occasionally farmers lose heavily by severe hailstorms, at the time when harvest is approaching, or very early frosts damage the grain, but crops may be insured in government-aided co-operative associations against the first disaster—which is usually very local when it occurs—and the farmer may secure himself against the worst effects of the second by the more general adoption of the combination of dairying or some other form of "mixed farming" with wheat-growing.

By the way, the little town of Red Deer is noted in agricultural circles from the fact that upon a farm near by was raised the "champion dairy cow" of Canada, rejoicing in the name of "Rosalind of Old Basing," which "surpassed in a twenty-four months' official test the previous highest butter record in Canada, by giving the milk equivalent of fourteen hundred and seventy-five pounds of butter."

Dairying was "a state-supervised industry" in days before Alberta attained provincial standing; now there is a provincial Dairy Commissioner, who, aided by a number of experts, assists the industry in a variety of ways; and there is at Calgary a government "dairy station," where butter is manufactured on the most approved lines from cream collected at fourteen co-operative creameries. But the numerous private creameries and cheese factories are by no means shut out from the benefits of expert aid and instruction, while a scheme of travelling dairies has been evolved to improve the output of butter made on the farms.

The Association of United Farmers of Alberta, like the Grain-Growers' Associations of Saskatchewan and Manitoba, is proving a power in influencing the public men of this largely agricultural province in the direction of reforms in the interests of farmers, with regard to the marketing and transportation of farm produce, the reduction in the prices of such articles of necessity to the farmer as binder twine, and the establishment of "elementary short course schools in agriculture."

Alberta has been the scene of interesting experiments (so far as Canada is concerned) of the effects of irrigation on a large scale in improving the fertility of the semi-arid districts in the south; and of the introduction of the Canadian Pacific Railway's system of "ready-made farms."

Irrigation on a small scale has long been carried on in Alberta, but there are great areas which can be successfully irrigated by means of large engineering works. To construct these, however, requires much capital; accordingly, the provincial government has thought it "in the general interest to dispose of extensive tracts of land to strong companies, on condition of their constructing a due proportion of irrigation works and supplying settlers with water on terms satisfactory to the government." The first corporation to irrigate on a large scale was the Alberta Land and Irrigation Company, which has two hundred and twenty miles of canals and dykes fed with water from the St. Mary's river, and upon its lands sugar-beets and alfalfa have been grown with great success. Another of these companies is the Southern Alberta Land Company, taking water from the Bow river, and the third, which has the largest irrigation scheme in America, is the Canadian Pacific Railway, and it is intended that its watercourses shall eventually supply about one million acres from the Bow river.

In this district the great railway has inaugurated the system of "ready-made farms" of from eighty to one hundred and sixty acres of irrigable, and one hundred and sixty to three hundred and twenty acres of non-irrigable land. The company erects a house and necessary buildings, sinks a well; fences, breaks, and sows part of the land and offers it to suitable settlers, requiring in payment only one-tenth of the price during the first year—chiefly payable after harvest. The remainder of the purchase money, with interest, is payable in instalments, of which the last is not required till the eleventh year. In allotting the farms, preference is given to men with families, and to help the newcomers to make the best of things under the unfamiliar conditions, the company has established "demonstration farms" in different districts.

The new arrivals in these districts have an advantage in social life and in the establishment of churches and schools over immigrants going singly into sparsely-settled regions; and any man with £400 or £500 of capital, who does not wish to "rough it," would do well to make careful inquiry about these farms. Some of the "ready-made farm" colonies have bought machines, and have worked in other ways, on a plan of co-operation, and there is great opportunity in these new communities for the successful application of the principle which combines "self-help" with very practical recognition of "one's duty to one's neighbour." Apart from this particular scheme, the man with capital may purchase improved or unimproved lands in Alberta from $15 (£3) to $35 (£7) the acre.

To the man with no capital, but a pair of willing hands, Alberta has free homesteads to offer (for conditions, see Appendix, Note B, page 160), and there is a good demand for labour, by which a thrifty newcomer can acquire a little capital before taking up land. On the farms, the monthly wages for a good single man (engaged by the year) range from $18 (£3 12*s.*) to $30 (£6), with board. When the engagement is for eight months they average from $25 (£5) to $40 (£8), whilst for harvesting and threshing the rate is from $35 (£7) to $50 (£10) the month.

At present, as in Manitoba and Saskatchewan, "hired men" sometimes find it difficult to obtain employment during the winter, and the farmers find it equally difficult (despite harvest excursions from the east) to get anything like the number of men they desire in the brief, hurried harvest. The more general adoption of intensive farming would greatly help to solve the labour problem. In the meantime the progressive farmer employs all the labour-saving machinery he can—in some cases, on the smaller farms, more than he can well afford.

About three-fifths of the self-supporting population of Alberta find employment in agriculture, leaving two-fifths to work in the factories, the mines, the shops, the transportation service, and in the several learned professions, and in all these lines of human energy there are opportunities awaiting the man who knows how to take advantage of them.

New lines are being built by each of the three great railway companies—the Canadian Pacific, the Canadian Northern, and the Grand Trunk Pacific—and the province, which thus will soon have two new gateways to the Western Ocean, is speculating eagerly on the probable effects of the opening of the Panama Canal.

Much labour is being expended (with excellent result on business and social conditions) on the provision of other means of transport and communication—roads and bridges, telegraphs and telephones. Many of the latter are rural, and are an especial boon to the women dwelling in the lonely little houses on the great farms. Some of these women, tied to their homes by the small children, whom they can neither leave nor take for long drives in cold weather, may not see another woman's face for weeks together; and in such cases it is a great thing to hear a friendly voice, and to know that, in case of emergency, doctor or nurse or other aid is within call.

HOT SULPHUR SPRING, BANFF, ALBERTA.

As for the schools and churches, conditions are much the same (except where the smaller "ready-made farms" give more chance of social life) as those in Saskatchewan; but in Alberta a school district may be formed for the benefit of eight instead of twelve children. Primary education is free and compulsory, but there is difficulty in obtaining a sufficient supply of teachers, and many of those now teaching have come from Eastern Canada, Great Britain, and the United States. The salaries paid are generally good, and the work of teaching a very small school is not arduous, unless, as sometimes happens, the children understand little or no English. Even in such a case, however, the children pick up the new language surprisingly quickly.

The University of Alberta, at Edmonton, has begun its work with the faculty of arts and applied science, but other departments will be added.

Alberta appears to be peculiarly rich in combustible materials beneath the soil. Coal of all grades, from lignite to anthracite, is found, and is mined at Bankhead and Canmore in the Rocky Mountains, at the Crow's Nest Pass, at Lethbridge, at Medicine Hat and near Edmonton. In 1911, one hundred and twenty collieries, with an output of three million tons, were in operation, employing about seven thousand workers. Coal may be bought at a very cheap rate at the pit's mouth, which is a great boon to settlers within reach of the mines. Natural gas and petroleum are also abundant in different parts of the province, from Medicine Hat to the Pelican river, far north of Edmonton. Once upon a time a "paying quantity" of gold used to be obtained from the Saskatchewan at Edmonton and other places, but, with the exception of coal, the chief mineral products at present being turned to account are its building stones and clay, which is being manufactured into brick at Calgary, Edmonton, and some smaller centres.

Calgary, with a population of considerably over sixty thousand, is the largest of Alberta's five cities; but Edmonton, in a more central position, is the capital, and now comes a good second in population, having recently absorbed the town of Strathcona, on the opposite side of the Saskatchewan. Much might be written of the numerous smaller towns and villages, which are nothing if not "progressive," but we must pass on, only stopping to remark that Alberta may also claim the epithet of "progressive"—especially from a political point of view—for the principles of co-operation, of public ownership of public utilities, and of taxing the land—not improvements—to prevent speculators holding it in idleness are in this province practised as well as preached.

XIV

BRITISH COLUMBIA, THE PACIFIC PROVINCE

THIS most westerly province of the Dominion makes a strong appeal to the imagination. Until the recent extension of Quebec and Ontario, British Columbia was the largest of the provinces, with its area of 395,000 square miles, or more than that of the British Isles, Italy, Denmark and Switzerland taken together. Of its sea of mountains, two hundred thousand square miles in extent, might be made twenty-four Switzerlands, but those who know the far-famed land of the European mountaineers are impressed with the fact that as yet man has gained no such hold upon the Rockies and the Selkirks and the Coast Ranges as upon the Alps. There are no picturesque châlets clinging to the sides of these Canadian mountains, and for the most part the snow-capped monarchs of the ranges lift up their heads from a land that seems almost as much outside the dominion of man as the blue heavens themselves.

On every hand "unconquered peaks" challenge the daring climber; and, hidden away amongst their recesses, lie lakes which seem the very acme of loneliness. The hunter, the scientist, the recluse, the seeker for adventure, can each strike out a trail for himself in British Columbia, or, if he so desires it, can shut himself up apart from other men in the wilderness of mountains; and sometimes stern necessity compels wild journeys through the unexplored maze of height and precipice and canyon.

Not long ago I heard of two men sent by a railway company across a mountain range to find—if they could—a possible pathway for the "iron horse" of civilization. For a hundred miles or more of unknown country their journey had to be performed on foot, with no hope of shelter or food save what they could carry with them. The former was represented by a frail tent of silk which could be thrust into a pocket, and the latter chiefly by beans sewn into narrow bags slung across their shoulders; for the food value of beans is high, and they dared not burden themselves with one ounce of superfluous comfort.

Romance is with us still, and, as Kipling suggests, may be found in "dock and deep and mine and mill"; nor does it need a poet to find it in the building of a railway, which here climbs by a corkscrew road up a forbidding mountain side, there plunges downward to the western ocean through a cut with which a tumultuous torrent has been busy for thousands of years.

It is just a hundred and twenty years since Alexander Mackenzie, one of the indomitable Scots who took up fur trading and exploring as their life-work, crossed the mountains from the east, and so with his party was the first to reach the Canadian Pacific coast overland. Others of his contemporaries and successors made memorable journeys down the furious rivers of the Pacific slope, and little by little gleaned some knowledge of the interior of the province, as, a few years earlier, Cook and Vancouver had begun to explore the inlets and the straits between the islands that for most of the way along the coast make a mighty breakwater against the ocean surges.

In natural beauty British Columbia is the most richly endowed of the provinces, for she possesses glorious forests and a picturesque sea-coast, in addition to the magnificent peaks and mountain lakes of gem-like colour and translucence, which she shares with her fair neighbour, Alberta. Her coast views are indeed the lovelier for the green heights springing from the water's edge, and for many a ghostly white peak gleaming in the distance, whilst in this province much of the "forest primeval" consists of Douglas firs, some towering up three hundred feet, and giant red cedars, with a girth at the butt of twenty or thirty feet, or even more. It was of these cedars, by the way, that the coast Indians made their huge, strangely-carved war-canoes, or dug-outs.

The climate of British Columbia, though having considerable variety in different districts, may appeal to some intending immigrants who dread cold. "The Coast," as Canadians of the prairie provinces often call it, gets the full benefit of the warm "Japanese current," and there winter comes chiefly in the guise of additional rain, while snow, if it does fall, does not lie long on the ground. British Columbia is, as was suggested in an earlier chapter, a land where roses of the types cultivated in English gardens bloom for many months in the year. In the uncleared woods, the undergrowth is a luxuriant tangle of shrubs and ferns and wild flowers; and gardens, if but a little neglected, run riot too. It is a wonderful thing, when travelling westward after crossing the prairies, where Nature appears to be rather insisting on the one idea of broad simplicity, and after plunging through the mountains, where she seems to invite your special attention to the magnificence of her backgrounds (though she herself has energy to spare for details too), to come down to this paradise of growing things, ranging from trees that tower to heaven to blossoms that climb on the houses, peep over grey walls and swing from the porches, bent apparently on breaking all bounds.

All the way up the coast of British Columbia and its adjacent islands the climate is "mild and moist"; and as far north as the new Grand Trunk Pacific port of Prince Rupert, which is indeed only in about the same latitude as Liverpool, severe cold need not be expected. Victoria, the capital, situated on Vancouver island, has a drier climate than the city of Vancouver, its younger and busier and more commercial rival on the mainland. But not all of the mainland has a damp climate. Behind the shelter of the coast range, which intercepts the warm moisture-laden winds from the West, lies a "dry belt," and between the coast mountains is many a pleasant sheltered valley rich in soil, mild, warm and prolific of fruit and other heat-loving crops.

PARLIAMENT HOUSE, VICTORIA.

During summer, in the Kootenay district, which lies in the south-east of the province, the temperature sometimes reaches eighty or ninety degrees in the shade, and in winter occasionally falls below zero, and the rainfall is usually sufficient to secure good crops of various descriptions; but much of the southern part of the interior of British Columbia consists of an elevated region, which, though deeply cut into by lakes and rivers, is described as a plateau, lying between mountain ranges on the east and west. It has an average altitude of three thousand five hundred feet, and here the rainfall is not superabundant. Indeed, in some districts irrigation is resorted to, with the result of great improvement in the crops. Altogether, however, there are many good farming and fruit districts in the valleys.

The Cariboo country, west and north of the Kootenay, has a more severe climate; but still further north lies the famous Peace River valley, partly in British Columbia and partly in Alberta, for which such great things are now being prophesied in agriculture. This region, though far north of Winnipeg, has a milder autumn and a shorter winter than Manitoba; and experts say that generally in the northern part of the province the clearing of the forests, which now prevent evaporation, will result in rendering milder the climate of this land of marsh and swamp and rigorous winter, which seems to resemble what the now progressive Germany was in the days of the Romans.

British Columbia has many rivers navigable in parts of their course, some of which, like the Columbia in the Kootenay, broaden into lakes, upon which ply quaint-looking, stern-paddle steamers drawing very little water. The Fraser, which rises in the Rocky Mountains and is navigable, though not uninterruptedly, for about six hundred miles, is the largest river, whose course is wholly within the province. It is a stream which every traveller on the Canadian Pacific Railway must remember, for the trains journey, for one hundred and thirty miles, with the rushing waters down the terrific, sharply-cut canyons, till, almost within sight of salt water, the river broadens into calm and the railway turns aside to reach Vancouver.

Far north, near Prince Rupert, the Skeena River, which is navigable for about seven months each year for two hundred miles from its mouth, enters the sea. It is the second in size of wholly British Columbian rivers, and is destined before long to become almost as well-known to travellers and tourists as the Fraser itself, for the Grand Trunk Pacific has taken advantage of the way it has cut through the mountains to gain the sea. Other notable rivers are the Thompson, the Naas and the Kootenay, within the province; and the Columbia, the Peace, the Stikine, and the Laird, which rise and flow within it for considerable distances, but pass beyond its boundaries before reaching the sea.

The rivers of British Columbia are swarming with fish, and so are the waters which wash the mainland coasts—some seven thousand miles in length, if the shores of inlets and bays are taken into account. In 1911-12 the value of the catch, amounting to over thirteen and a half million dollars, exceeded that of the preceding year by four and a half millions, and for the first time British Columbia was the leading province of the Dominion in the fisheries. She owes her supremacy in this respect to salmon, though vast numbers of halibut, herring, sturgeon and other varieties of fish are taken in her waters. Amongst these are the oolachan or candle fish, a small oily fish from which the Indians make a substitute for butter.

Much of British Columbia's catch of herrings goes to China, and some of her sturgeon are sent, strange to say, to her great rival in the fisheries, Nova Scotia. As for her salmon, when canned it goes all over the world. Chinamen do much work in the salmon canneries and a machine recently introduced is known as "the Iron Chink," from the fact that it does the work of many Chinamen in cleaning and cutting the fish. Lobsters are not found in British Columbian waters, but crabs and shrimps and prawns are plentiful. The Japanese do much fishing along the coasts, and from Vancouver many of their gasoline launches go out. A whaling company which uses fast steamers and machine guns has several stations on Vancouver Island; and parts of the monsters, taken chiefly for the sake of the whalebone and oil, are exported as food to Japan.

I have, however, begun to discuss the great groups of industries at the wrong end. Important and rapidly increasing as are the fisheries of this ocean-washed province, the value of their annual product is at present far surpassed by that of the mines, then of the forests, and thirdly, by that of the farms and orchards taken together.

The discovery of gold played a great part in the making of the province. In the earlier decades of the nineteenth century British Columbia was occupied only by the Indians and by the traders of the Hudson Bay Company, with posts scattered at wide intervals through the wilderness. About 1839 a few Scotch and Canadian farmers were brought out to supply the traders with some of the necessaries that had hitherto been brought round by Cape Horn from England.

Meanwhile, the United States was casting envious eyes on the country; but after noisy demands on the part of some Americans for the whole coast as far north as the Alaskan boundary, it was agreed by the Treaty of Oregon in 1846 that the 49th parallel of north latitude should be the mainland boundary, and that the whole of the island of Vancouver should remain under the British flag.

In 1849 that great island was granted to the Hudson Bay Company, on condition that they should bring in settlers. The conditions were not fulfilled, and as late as 1854 there were scarcely five hundred white people on the island, including the traders; but in 1857 it became known that gold had been discovered along some of the rivers of the mainland (New Caledonia, as it was then called), and in the following spring thousands of prospectors arrived at Victoria. The little town was soon surrounded by an encampment of rude huts and tents, and the newcomers swarmed across to the new "Eldorado" in all kinds of craft, some paying for their temerity with their lives.

The rush of gold seekers caused the government to try to open roads to the mining country, and the traveller on the railway through the Thompson and Fraser valleys catches many a glimpse of the old "Cariboo road," sometimes clinging to the cliff as much as a thousand feet above the water. This road has been practically abandoned since the opening of the railway; but now government is again occupied with the project of a highway from Alberta to the Pacific coast.

In the first decade, after the rush to the "diggings" began, about fifty million dollars' worth of the precious metal was obtained in the Cariboo and Cassiar country, and still gold is being obtained there by more scientific methods of working. There are also valuable deposits of silver, lead, copper, zinc, coal, building stone and brick clay, all of which are worked more or less; and the different mining camps employ a large number of men. The value of the mining output for 1912 was about thirty-two and a half million dollars.

This was followed pretty closely by the value of the lumber of the year, which equalled $28,000,000 (£5,600,000). The forest area, including that covered by small trees, has been estimated at over one hundred and eighty-two million acres. Along the coast and up the river valleys of the mainland and on Vancouver island are many magnificent trees. The most valuable commercially are Douglas fir, cypress, red cedar, white spruce and western hemlock. On the coast the trees are larger than further inland; and it is said that the climate is so favourable to their growth that they increase in size very much more rapidly than in most other parts of America. British Columbia, like other provinces, has begun to realize the immense value of its forests, and is taking steps to preserve them, but about a third of the "cut" of the Dominion comes from this province, and thousands of men find employment in the woods and the saw mills.

Not many years ago the agricultural possibilities of this region were scarcely regarded seriously, but it has a splendid home market for all the products of the farm; and last year the value of the agricultural produce (including fruit, of which British Columbia is beginning to make a specialty) was equal to more than three-quarters of the lumber output. But this is only a beginning. A recent estimate gives the area of known cultivable land at twenty-four million acres, of which about ten millions is in the Peace River country, but hardly one-eighth of this land is at present in use, and much of the interior of the country is practically unexplored. There are districts in the Kootenay, about the Okanagan lake, in the neighbourhood of New Westminster, upon Vancouver island and in some other regions, which are fairly well settled, and in these is grown a vast quantity of beautiful apples and other fruit. In fact, fruit is the greatest agricultural product of British Columbia, and last year the yield of the orchards and fruit "ranches" was estimated at $14,000,000, or about equal to that of the fisheries. This is the only farm product which at present goes out of the province; but the estimated value of cereals, beef, dairy produce and all the other miscellaneous yield of the farms accounted only for another eight million dollars. Government is making efforts in various ways to stimulate agriculture. For instance, it aids the establishment of co-operative creameries; but millions of dollars are spent annually outside the province for meat, cheese, butter, poultry, eggs and articles of food, which might well be supplied from the prolific soil of British Columbia were there only more hands to work it.

At present, however, this province is in the somewhat peculiar and unsatisfactory position of having a mere fraction of its people (one-quarter) living on the land. The population was put down in the last census year as 392,480 (of whom the males were in excess of the females by nearly one hundred and eleven thousand),

and of this number the two cities of Vancouver and Victoria accounted for over one hundred and fifty thousand. Now these cities, with their suburbs, are said to have a population of two hundred thousand, or nearly half the total for the province.

Both Vancouver and Victoria are already extremely important ports, and expect much additional ocean trade when the Panama Canal is opened. The northern port of Prince Rupert is also busy, although the railway, of which it is the terminal, is not yet completed. There are many other ports and inland towns; mining, railway construction, and lumbering camps all needing supplies; and the man who understands dairying or market-gardening or fruit growing has a choice of opportunities in British Columbia.

In the Peace River district is a block of Dominion lands which may be taken up by homesteaders on the same terms as the free grants in the other western provinces. (See Appendix, pg. 160, Note B.) A strip of land twenty miles wide on each side of the Canadian Pacific Railway main line belongs to the crown, and until December, 1911, was administered by the Minister of the Interior at Ottawa, but is now under the management of the provincial government.

Provincial crown lands are offered for sale at from $5 (£1) to $10 (£2) the acre, or for lease for cutting hay or other purposes. They may be pre-empted by settlers—in which case there are conditions of improvement and residence, in addition to the payment of $1 (4*s.* 2*d.*) per acre in four equal annual instalments. Pre-emptions are limited to one hundred and sixty acres of agricultural lands, and no one may hold more than one claim at a time; nor can an alien obtain title deeds for a pre-emption; but anyone desiring full and reliable information as to how to obtain provincial land should write to the Chief Commissioner of Lands, Victoria, British Columbia.

The Canadian Pacific Railway and other companies and private persons also offer unimproved or improved agricultural lands for sale at prices ranging from $5 (£1) the acre up to $500 (£100) for irrigated land in a good situation, while bearing orchards may cost as much as from $1,000 (£200) to $12,000 (£2,400) an acre.

By clauses recently added to the land regulations of British Columbia it is provided that any self-supporting woman over eighteen years of age (except a wife living with her husband) may pre-empt one hundred and sixty acres of agricultural land on the same conditions as men; and this provision is made applicable to deserted wives, and women whose husbands have not contributed to their support for two years, as well as to spinsters and widows.

It is most important, however, that it should be understood that the agricultural lands available for pre-emption or purchase direct from the government are situated almost entirely in districts difficult of access and ill-provided with roads and bridges, whilst a considerable amount of capital is necessary for the purchase of good land in well-settled districts.

The government of British Columbia reserves one-quarter of all town sites and of lands divided into small lots (of one acre or less), and these are usually sold by public auction.

LUMBERING IN BRITISH COLUMBIA.

It seems very natural that along the coast and amongst the mountains the population should be gathered into centres, larger or smaller, where they can enjoy some of the comforts of civilized life unattainable by isolated settlers, and the practice certainly has its advantages with regard to social and church life, and the education of the young. In British Columbia, by the way, free government schools are established where twenty children between the ages of six and sixteen can be brought together. In 1912 there were 538 schools in operation, including twenty-three high schools. At Vancouver there is a provincial Normal School; also a number of private schools and colleges; while the Vancouver and Victoria colleges are in affiliation with McGill University, Montreal, and provision has been made for the endowment of a university of British Columbia, by the setting apart of two million acres of public lands.

Men of small capital are strongly advised to go in for "intensive" culture of a small farm, rather than to attempt to take a large piece of land or to devote themselves solely to fruit culture, for orchards in bearing are expensive, and to wait for returns till a newly-planted orchard becomes productive is also costly; but quick returns can be obtained from the keeping of poultry and pigs, and the growing of early vegetables for a town or mining camp.

Small holdings simplify the labour problem, which is acute in British Columbia, and complicated by the difficulties attendant on Oriental labour. This is much employed, in spite of the feeling that, for the sake of Canada's future, the unrestricted admission of Orientals would be a grave mistake. That is a question, however, which it does not belong to the purpose of this book to discuss.

XV

THE YUKON AND NORTH-WEST TERRITORIES

NORTH of British Columbia lies the Yukon territory, which about sixteen years ago suddenly became interesting to the world on account of the discoveries of gold on two streams flowing into the Klondyke. This is itself a tributary of the Yukon river, which is navigable for over sixteen hundred miles in its course from White Horse, through the territory bearing its own name and through Alaska, to the Behring Sea. There is no need to write of the stampede to the Klondyke in the late nineties. The production of gold in the Yukon gradually declined after 1901, but mining is still its chief industry, and the introduction of more elaborate methods of mining are now again increasing the output. The territory is rich also in copper and coal, both of which are being mined with success. There is a good local market for coal at Dawson, which, founded in 1896, had at one time a population of twenty thousand. This had fallen by 1911 to four thousand, however.

The climate is very severe in winter, especially during January and February, and in the northern part of the district the ground never thaws for more than a foot in depth; but the surface thaws, and only a few miles south of the Arctic Circle the summer climate is said to be pleasant, and hardy vegetables such as turnips and cabbages can be grown.

Just beyond the borders of the Yukon district, on the banks of the Mackenzie river, stands the most northerly of the Hudson Bay Company's posts—Fort McPherson. It has been described as "truly an Arctic village. The sun never sets for about six weeks in summer, and is constantly below the horizon for the same time in winter." It is visited by the Eskimos of the shores of the Arctic Ocean and by the whalers, chiefly from San Francisco.

Several years ago the whole whaling fleet was entrapped by the ice, and its crews obliged to go into winter quarters at Herschel Island. Here there is a detachment of the Mounted Police, who have to face all kinds of difficulty and danger in keeping order and doing their duty—often of a humanitarian character—in the northern wildernesses. Usually they carry through their undertakings with marked success, but occasionally they are the victims, or the heroes of a tragedy.

In winter a small body of the police make a regular patrol from Dawson to Fort McPherson and back; but in 1911 the patrol did not return, when expected, and its four members, having "failed to make the pass over the mountains," were found dead in the snow, but one day's march from safety.

Amongst the resources of this wild north land, besides its mineral wealth, of which no doubt a very small proportion is yet discovered, is its excellent fish—white fish, Arctic trout, the "inconnu" (peculiar to the Mackenzie river, and so named by Mackenzie's party), and salmon of numerous varieties. It is also likely to remain for generations to come the hunting ground of the fur trader, for wild animals, large and small, abound; and if the land proves of value for little else, its fur-bearing animals—especially if some measures should be taken to preserve and protect them—will be an increasing source of wealth to the Dominion.

As for the inhabitants of the land, there are several tribes of Indians and Eskimos speaking different tongues, whilst the white race—apart from the miners and business men of the Yukon—is represented chiefly by traders and missionaries. For several generations the Roman Catholic and Anglican missionaries have been doing brave work in the frozen north, and a large proportion of the Indians have embraced Christianity in one form or the other.

But we must pass on, for this portion of Canada cannot be said to offer large opportunity as a field for British immigration, though it has been a field where Britons, as explorers or heralds of the Cross, have again and again proved their kinship to the Norse heroes of older days.

XVI

THE MAN WHOM CANADA NEEDS

HITHERTO, in our progress through the Dominion and its provinces, I have been trying to show what Canada has to offer to the newcomer; and if I were asked to sum it up in one word—it would be that word which has been already used so frequently in the pages of this book—"opportunity!" But I wish to devote the remainder of this volume to the immigrant himself (or herself), first discussing the type Canada needs and desires; and secondly, making a few suggestions which, I hope (with vivid recollections of what it means even under favourable conditions to be a new arrival in a strange land), may be of real help to the immigrant.

To the self-respecting man or woman there is probably nothing more attractive about the Dominion as a field for immigration than the fact that this great promising young nation does *need* immigrants. What can be more depressing to anyone than the sense of being a superfluous member of the human family—a person whom no one really wants—a worker regarded chiefly in the light of an occupier of a position keenly desired by someone else?

But Canada absolutely needs more human beings, and, above all, she needs workers. Let no one mistake, however. She does not need, and if by the most careful sifting of the newcomers she can prevent it, she will not have drones in her hive—unless, indeed, they come well-provided with the honey prepared by the workers. In other words, of course, the man who has more or less capital finds it easy enough to gain admittance to the Dominion, and may even continue to live in idleness therein. This is a fact accomplished to the scorn of his neighbours, by many a "remittance-man" in east or west, who has had the ill-luck to be provided with just money enough to enable him to evade the Scriptural dictum: "If any man will not work, neither shall he eat;" but, of course, the overwhelmingly large number of Canada's immigrants are not burdened with any superfluity of worldly gear.

THE FISH MARKET, VANCOUVER.

The much-talked-of "opportunity," moreover, is not (is it necessary to state the fact?) opportunity to pick up gold in the streets, or to win a fortune without labour. In isolated cases, men have gained wealth with surprising rapidity by some piece of luck, or special business astuteness, but opportunity for the ordinary man means a probability—amounting almost to a certainty—that good, honest, intelligent work in any one of a wide range of different lines will receive its due reward. It means also that for the man with a little more than the average energy and ability and insight there are in this new land, with its frequent changes of conditions, its constant opening out of new regions and of hitherto unused natural resources, many more chances of "making good" than under the more stereotyped conditions of older countries.

The man whom Canada needs is strong and healthy, preferably young enough to be readily adaptable to new conditions, sound in mind and well taught, trained and educated. The man she desires most of all is one of the good blood of the British Isles, imbued with love for the old flag of the Empire, and for the ancient traditions of his race; one who will help in the building up of Canada on the same lines as those on which the work has been begun—as a free British nation within the Empire; one, in short, who is adapted by heredity, education and previous history to understand this ideal of nationhood, and to take his place in the furtherance of it.

Good British immigrants are the more needed—to aid in leavening the whole lump—because to-day Canada is the goal for people of many races and languages, who, in most instances, have everything to learn of the institutions and the ideals of the nation, which (according to laws perhaps too speedily allowing to foreign men a voice in the affairs of the country) they will soon be helping to mould. That the problem is serious will be seen from the fact that, according to the figures of 1911-12, and apart from the English-speaking immigrants from the United States, more than one immigrant in each four that year was a foreigner in birth and speech, and in some years the proportion of foreigners has been higher. The immigration of the afore-mentioned year represented no less than sixty-five nationalities in all, including Ruthenians, Bulgarians, Chinese, Hebrews, Italians, Finns, Scandinavians—literally by the thousand.

There are whole districts in the West largely settled by groups of foreigners. For instance, in Saskatchewan, between Saskatoon and Prince Albert, the Canadian Northern Railway runs through a region which, though colonized in part by English-speaking people, is dotted with foreign settlements. Amongst these are the quaint community villages, built of mud, of that Quaker-like Russian sect, the Doukhobors. Some of their number gave at one time considerable trouble to the authorities, and endangered their own lives by going on strange pilgrimages in the depths of a Saskatchewan winter to seek for Christ, Whom they believed to have returned to earth; but in general they are a quiet, inoffensive, cleanly, honest people. In the same district are many Galicians, less remarkable for cleanliness and sobriety of demeanour than the Doukhobors, and often living in small mud huts thatched with straw, which, though of picturesque exterior, are often ill-ventilated and ill-kept within.

The schools, however, are rapidly making "Canadians" of the younger generation—in speech, and perhaps to a certain extent in ideas.

The prairies have also their Icelandic and Norwegian and Swedish settlers, who are generally credited with being of an excellent type. Then in the cities and in the railway construction camps are Italians, somewhat quarrelsome and ready to use their knives amongst themselves, but excellent workers in all the digging and delving necessary for the making of a railway line or preparing for the foundations of some great new building. It is said to be the ambition of many an Italian to become the owner of a fruit store, and to judge by the numbers of such little shops in every city—over whose treasures of apples and oranges and bananas a dark-eyed woman or child is keeping guard—it must be an ambition often fulfilled.

It is odd, indeed, how the different nationalities seem to have such strong predilections for particular trades. Every considerable centre of population in Canada must surely have its Chinese laundries, very numerous in the large towns. The Chinese, too, go into business as restaurant keepers, or keepers of tea and curiosity shops; and in the West they enter domestic service in private houses or hotels. But one never sees a Chinaman engaged in the rag-and-bottle-collecting business, for instance. Indeed, that occupation seems to be left wholly to the Jews; while the porters on the Pullman cars are nearly always negroes, with an occasional Jap on the western lines.

It is often said that much of the hardest and heaviest work in city and mine and railway making is done by foreigners. In that respect alone the country owes them a real debt; but there is no doubt that the bar of differing language and customs prevents Canada getting the best contributions to her total strength from the little-understood and often-misunderstood foreigners. As time goes on the Canadians may be more successful than hitherto in bridging the gulf that separates them from the newcomers of alien speech, but at present the tendency is for the foreigners to cluster together in certain districts in the country—certain quarters in the cities—where it is difficult to reach them with Canadianizing influences. In unskilled labour and in some more skilled trades they are formidable competitors to the newcomer from the British Isles. But in a measure—because of their coming in such numbers—the Briton is all the more the man Canada wants; and it is satisfactory that the proportion of British-born to the whole number of immigrants has of late tended to rise. During the decade ending March, 1912, the British immigrants outnumbered the foreign-born by nearly 300,000. This is leaving the newcomers from the United States out of account; but they also outnumbered the foreigners.

As has been stated already, the man wanted most of all is the man willing to go on the land. Every province, from Nova Scotia in the east to British Columbia in the west, has land waiting for the farmer, the market gardener and the fruit grower.

In this connection it may be mentioned, that it is not necessary for any one to pay a premium for a youth to "learn farming" in Canada. If he is willing to work and of at least ordinary intelligence, however inexperienced he may be, a lad can earn his board and lodging and at least a few dollars during the busy months; and the money spent on the premium had far better be laid by to help the boy in starting for himself later. Usually the promised instruction in farming is given in much the same fashion as when a big boy begins to teach a little one to swim, by pushing him somewhat violently into the water. The farm pupil is plunged into any work at which he can be made useful, the farmer trusting to his learning the business by practising it; and usually he does learn much in this way. If possible, however, it is well for a boy thinking of farming in Canada to learn how to milk, and to attend to a horse before coming out. Milking is an especially useful accomplishment, and may very much aid him in getting a good situation and fair wages.

If the newcomer is young, even though he may already be possessed of some capital, it is often a good plan for him to take a situation for a short time as "a hired man," in the region where he proposes to settle, with a view to getting into the ways of the country; learning how best to adapt himself to prevalent conditions, including those of climate; and also how to estimate properly the values of land and stock in that particular district.

A man does not need to fear that he will lose socially by working for a farmer, for, in the country, little attention is paid to the arbitrary social distinctions of older lands, and in most farmhouses a willing, obliging, courteous, adaptable "hired man" is trusted much like one of the family. Sometimes, indeed, it is difficult for him to fit happily into his strange environment; and there are cases (the facts must be faced) where a mean master endeavours to take advantage of the newcomer's ignorance. In general, however, a man who is willing to work, is of good manners and character, and is not ashamed to learn will be treated with respect and kindness. In fact, his value will be speedily recognized, for there are two sides to this question, and the ideal "hired man" is perhaps as rare as the ideal employer.

In the towns, especially in the older provinces, social conditions are more similar to those of England, and it is often asked what a man does and who his father was as well as what he is. Even in the centres of population, however, the way of a young man of character to a position of influence and comfort is more easily found than "at home." No doubt the free educational system of Canada is a check on the snobbish spirit; for in their school days, at least, the children of the village magnate and of the most prosperous farmer of the neighbourhood meet on equal terms with those of the hired man, the mechanic, or the doer of odd jobs.

In after life this early lesson, that quality in muscle or brain or moral character does not depend upon class or length of purse, can never be quite forgotten; and it may often happen that the clever, industrious son of some poor man may climb to a position in the community to which his former school mates, though sons of the richest man in the village, can only look up. And, if the poor man's son never climbs, he comforts himself with the reflection that "Jack is as good as his master," which is an assertion sometimes open to question.

However, the practical application of all this to the immigrant, even though he may belong to the class which prides itself on good birth and good breeding, is that in Canada, especially in the country, no honest work will injure his position in the eyes of his neighbours. The point that counts for or against him is—will he work? or does he think it more "gentlemanly" to waste his time and strength and money with other idle young men of kindred spirit? The fact is, that while the Mother-isles have sent of their best to Canada, they have sent also many a useless scamp. It has been well suggested that the friends of such ne'er-do-wells ought not to imagine that transplanting "a poor stick" to "the colonies" will necessarily change its nature. If the young man's misfortune is lack of ability or character, he stands more chance in Canada of disgracing the name of Englishman than of doing anything else; but if his lack is merely the wherewithal to start in farming, or business, or to obtain a college education in England, it is well worth while to try sending him to Canada.

I know men, some British, some Canadians, who have had the force to work their way through every difficulty to satisfactory positions; and what one has done another may do. For instance, the ranks of the ministry in all the churches, though in some cases they may obtain help from bursaries in the theological colleges, are largely recruited from those who have had their own way to make; and have been obliged to earn the money to pay for their college expenses. Sometimes, indeed, the student may have had to stop midway in his course to make money enough to finish it. It is the same with all the learned professions—many men "put themselves through" the university and are probably none the worse for the battle.

Now here, I believe, is a chance for some of the lads who come out from the "Old Country" in early youth, either alone or with their parents. Amongst the men whom Canada needs are earnest, Christian ministers to work in her wide land amongst all the scattered peoples—foreigners, British immigrants and native Canadians; but perhaps it is scarcely necessary to say that this is not an avenue to wealth; and the man who adopts the ministry as a profession must be actuated by a higher motive than ambition. She needs, too, men who will make a life-work of teaching, a profession which in Canada is largely left to women, in spite of (or it may be partly because of) the fact that men are paid about twice as much as women of the same standing and for the same work.

Rates of wages are, of course, much higher in town than country; but rents and living are high in proportion. For example, take the case of a married man with a family. If willing to work on a farm, he may get an engagement by the year at from \$20 (£4) to \$30 (£6) the month (the wages varying considerably in different parts of the country), whilst the unskilled worker in the city will get probably from \$1·50 (6s.) to \$2·50 (10s.) for a ten-hour day; but the former may count on steady work and a free house with a garden, and also on some such extras as milk, vegetables or apples; while the townsman may frequently lose some days' pay on account of bad weather and have to disburse a very high proportion of his earnings as rent. Moreover, if there are children to consider, the advantages of the country compared to the town are great both with regard to health of body and of mind.

There are other possibilities in the country besides work on the farms. For instance, there is a demand for skilled workers in cheese factories, creameries, and so forth; and it seems to me that there would be a good opening in many a village for a man who had in his fingers some such trade as that of a shoemaker or harness maker. Often the country people have to take articles that need repairing to a distant town because there is no capable workman in the village where they go for their "mail" or groceries. If such a man had a taste for country life, he could often get a small house and a good garden cheap; and in the farmer's busy seasons could, if he chose, add to his income by doing outdoor work at good wages. In this way he might soon be able to own his own house, paying for it in instalments; but, indeed, in some of the cities—Toronto, for instance—a thrifty working man often speedily saves enough to make the small first payment necessary to buy a house, and then gradually works off the remainder of the debt. Others buy lots on the outskirts of the town and put up for themselves small "shacks," which they transform bit by bit into comfortable little houses.

But there are numerous evidences that in other lines than farming the British immigrant is needed, and can, under ordinarily fortunate circumstances, with industry and thrift, prove himself to be of value to Canada. For instance, it is noticeable that the first of the Imperial Home Reunion Associations was founded in Winnipeg by business men who believed that it would be for the advantage of the Dominion if the numerous British workmen employed in the cities and towns could immediately have their wives and children with them, instead of having to send money over to the "Old Country" for their support. This step would not have been taken had not the workmen in question proved their value. Another evidence is that of one's senses. Alike in the far West, and in centrally-situated Toronto, one cannot enter a store or a street car without hearing voices that one recognizes as those of comparatively recent arrivals from Britain. These have obtained situations in a great variety of occupations; and if one sends for a gardener, a plumber, or a paperhanger to work about one's house, it seems that every other man in such trades is English.

The Dominion government confines its direct invitations to immigrants to "farmers, farm labourers and domestic servants," all of whom belong to classes singularly little troubled by fear of competition; but the Provincial governments sometimes venture to give a broader invitation. For instance, in a letter recently received from Mr. Arthur S. Barnstead, Secretary of the Department of Industries and Immigration of the province of Nova Scotia, it is stated that "the industrial expansion upon which Nova Scotia has entered has created a strong demand for industrial workers. Many of our plants have been unable to secure the necessary number of native workers, and thus have been compelled to engage British and foreign labour. Miners have been imported for our coal mines, iron workers for our steel works, as well as textile and other tradespeople. Last year, in the occupations taken up by the English-speaking newcomers to Nova Scotia, mining came first (numerically), though farming followed closely; and the list of 2,736 persons includes, besides "housewives" and children, craftsmen, tradesmen, clerks, professional men, soldiers, and others."

Rapid industrial expansion is proceeding in other provinces, with a consequent demand for workers of all classes, and altogether, I am sure that the British immigrant of the right stamp—used to work and not expecting to get "good money" without giving a due equivalent for it—may find many an opening in Canada—in the cultivation of the soil, or in some other of the numerous occupations which civilized man has devised for himself. But there comes from British Columbia the warning, which may apply to other provinces also, that "the man without a trade, the clerk, the accountant and the semi-professional" has not a good chance for employment, unless he will do manual work in an emergency, or has means of support "for six months in a year while seeking a situation."

XVII

THE WOMAN CANADA NEEDS

JUDGING by statistics, it may be averred that Canada needs women in general, especially in some districts, even more than men. At any rate, according to the census taken in 1911 there was, in a total population of a little over seven millions, an excess of males over females of four hundred and thirty-seven thousand, and as each year the immigration returns show the arrival of more men than women (the figures for 1911 were 211,266 males and 82,922 females), the disproportion between the sexes is growing continually greater; but it cannot be said that at present the Dominion makes the same effort to attract women as men. For instance, the bonus given to booking agents is less on a woman than a man, and the only way in which a woman can acquire a free grant of Dominion crown lands is in the character of a widowed mother of a child, or children, under eighteen years of age.

Possibly this inequality of opportunity has arisen from the notion that a woman is not suited for doing homestead duties—and many women are not—but as a matter of fact the wife of a struggling newcomer is often left alone for weeks at a time on the homestead, while her husband "hires himself out" to a farmer, or works on a new railway. In British Columbia, as already mentioned, a woman may take up a pre-emption, which is practically the same—so far as the obligations of residence and cultivation are concerned—as the Dominion free grants.

It must, I think, be frankly admitted that the isolation of the life in many instances either on a homestead or on a great Western farm is hard for the woman. Some little time since I met a bright young woman, with one small girl of four or five, who was thankfully travelling south to Vancouver from an island in the neighbourhood of Prince Rupert, where for a considerable part of two years she had been living on a pre-emption whilst her husband had been away working on the new railway. She told me that, with the exception of one solitary young man—a neighbouring homesteader—she had had no neighbour nearer than three miles away, and that there had been days during the two years when she had been so ill that she could not leave her bed to give bread to the little one, who, scarcely out of babyhood, had had to be sent herself to the "bread box" to get something to eat. Such a story seems suggestive of possible tragedy, but the woman did not dwell on what might have been, but rejoiced simply in the fact that the hard task was over, and that, largely through her effort, they had the patent for the land, which now they would be able to sell if they could find a purchaser.

THE SASKATCHEWAN RIVER AT EDMONTON, ALBERTA.

I could not help thinking that one quality of the woman that Western Canada needs is courage, and another is resourcefulness; and perhaps if I repeat here the story told me by the wife of a successful pioneer farmer in Saskatchewan, it may help, more than any generalities, to give an idea of a woman's lot on a prairie farm. Mrs. Smith—as I will call her—had gone as a bride to a little house of one lower room (fourteen feet by sixteen) and a half storey upstairs. She, by the way, had spent her girlhood in the West, and perhaps knew from experience how to manage under circumstances which would have sorely tried an Englishwoman of her class.

The tiny dwelling, lined with building paper and thin boards, was not plastered for a year or two and at first the one room was kitchen, dining-room and washhouse. The house was a full mile from the next one, and stood in the centre of a great field of wheat, which sometimes, when the babies (who soon arrived) began to toddle, seemed to the young mother to grow perilously high, for she had heard stories of little ones wandering off into the tall wheat and being lost.

The coming of the little ones to a pioneer woman is often a terrible test of courage and endurance, for it is hard to get either doctor or experienced nurse at the right time. Sometimes the prospective mother goes into town to a hospital or to some friend; but generally she stays at home. The neighbours do the best they can, and often all goes well—and sometimes it does not. In such a case and in many another emergency the rural telephone is a wonderful boon and comfort—and may be even counted a life-saving agency. Incidentally, I may mention that women, competent to take care of mother and infant or to help in case of sickness, who would be willing to take charge also of the domestic arrangements of a little house, while its mistress was incapacitated, would not be likely to lack work in the West. Many people, who could hardly meet the high charges for a regularly trained nurse, would be glad to pay well for such services. Mrs. Smith told me, however, that it was practically impossible to get help, and that a neighbour had driven hither and thither for a week in a vain search for someone to take care of his wife, at last getting an old woman from the immigrant shed in a somewhat distant town. My informant's impression was that there was "a great chance" for "hired girls" in these prairie communities, for on the farms they are treated like "one of the family." Nevertheless they generally prefer to stay in the towns.

Gradually things improve as the neighbourhoods get settled, though the great farms of the exclusively wheat-growing districts "make few neighbours." The more so, because many a Western farmer develops a passion for adding field to field—or "quarter-section to quarter-section." The Smith farm, for instance, grew to be "seven miles" round; and the husband was often working a mile away from home, but after the first few years he managed to get a man and his wife to live on the farm. Despite the isolation, Mrs. Smith did not regard the life as a hard one. She "liked the farm very much," she said, and thought the women in the West had "easier times" than those in the East, for the regular "hired men" lived in the bunk-house, though they came to the house for their meals, and after the first two years she did not have to cook for the harvesters and threshers, whose meals were provided from "a cook car." She was, however, fortunate in having a husband who was both considerate and capable.

As to the social aspects of life, she had been used in her girlhood, though that, too, was spent on a prairie farm—near Regina—to go out a great deal in the evenings "with her musical brothers" to meet other young people, and no doubt she felt the change to the new district, where, of the few women who could be counted neighbours, some were very rough. But soon there were alleviations. From the first there was a church only five miles away, and later there were services in the school-house, which, by the way, in that section at least was very much of a social centre.

Mrs. Smith usually boarded the lady who taught there, and the section had "fine teachers," who brought on the little flocks of from sixteen to twenty-six children most successfully, lent books to the readers of the community and got up the summer picnics in connection with the school—the more enjoyed, perhaps, because other entertainments were so few and far between. These consisted of a Sunday school Christmas tree, an occasional concert, or a public dance to which "nice women" did not go—at least, in that particular district—as it was open to everyone who could pay, and was attended by men of the rougher sort, who thought it impossible to enjoy themselves without much whiskey.

By the help of the neighbours, the mail was usually brought from the post office, ten miles distant, three times a week, and the Smiths subscribed for several magazines and newspapers. The telephone, when it came, was "a great help"; but, when "the children began to want to see people" and to need somewhat better education than could be gained in the little country school, this family moved into one of the gay, bustling little prairie towns. Mrs. Smith's experience, it must be remembered, was that of a pioneer, and there are districts in the provinces where that kind of life is becoming a thing of the past, though pioneers are still plentiful.

In the particular town to which the Smiths moved (and I have reason to believe it not exceptional) there is a high proportion of young people in the population and brides are often numerous, whose trousseaux are, perhaps, accountable for setting the pace in a style of dressing which is costly, and which seems almost incongruously handsome in comparison with the tiny houses in which many of the young couples dwell. But money is easily earned and quickly spent by the eager optimistic Westerner; and, doubtless, if domestic servants were easier to get and to keep, more well-to-do folk would turn their attention to building larger houses.

In the rural districts of the older provinces there are plenty of somewhat isolated farmhouses; but there are also many farming communities where the families are close enough together to enjoy a good deal of social life; and where this is the case the country life is a delightful one, for young folk especially. The boys and girls on the farms learn early to do the work of men and women; but it is work which, if not overdone in amount, is healthful for mind and body; and the informal country merry-makings have a charm of their own.

A sleigh ride of several miles, on a moonlight night, through a lovely snow-covered landscape of hill and woods and valley, does not detract from the enjoyment of an informal carpet dance, especially when the vehicle is a big box sleigh, filled with a dozen lively lads and lasses, whose songs and laughter ring out above the jingling bells. A wedding feast or a barn-raising bee, a church social, or a school concert, a "strawberry festival" or a "Christmas tree"—country folk know how to enjoy all these things; as they enjoy chance meetings in the store or at the church door—and now there are in most provinces Farmers' Clubs and Women's Institutes to aid in the good work of drawing together country neighbours of all the different denominations. Above all, the country is the place for the little ones, where they may spend their first years amongst the animals and birds and flowers, which the normal child loves, leading a simple, outdoor life.

But one of the needs of Canada is more women (she has some already) who shall appreciate the country and know how to make the best of it for themselves, their families and their neighbours. She wants women of any race, British or foreign, who are strong enough and wise enough to discover ways of developing the fine possibilities of country life, and counteracting any tendency towards its degeneration into dulness and stagnation. To-day the trend of the population of this new and supposedly agricultural country citywards is a fact which is at once remarkable and rather disquieting. Perhaps it is due in part to "the earth hunger" that besets many a farmer, and inclines him to sacrifice to it the comfort of his family and the possibilities of congenial society. Whatever its cause, women may, perhaps, do quite as much as men to stem the current and make country life what it ought to be.

The woman Canada asks for, by the official voice of the Dominion Immigration Department, is the domestic servant, and when necessary the government assists the girl with a loan of £4 for her passage money. Now there is no question that from coast to coast there is a demand for the woman who will help with domestic work. A healthy, intelligent, industrious girl, if she has had any experience in general housework, can command wages of from $10 (£2) to $16 (£8 4*s.*) a month in the East up to $80 in the West, in both cases with room and board included, whilst a housekeeper or a competent cook gets $30 (£6) or $35 (£7) or even more. For domestic servants the demand is practically unlimited both in town and country. The wages are not quite so high in the rural districts, but in many cases the girl in farm and country houses is treated like a member of the family, so far at least as having her meals with her employers; and not infrequently a good girl is actually treated like a daughter of the house, taking her share in whatever little festivities there may be.

Perhaps, however, an "Old-Country" girl, brought up amongst the servant-keeping instead of the service-giving class, and coming to Canada to act as "home-help" or "lady-help," is sometimes deceived into expecting too much by the phrase of "being treated like one of the family." In the first place, if, as sometimes happens, the mistress, who unreservedly treats her domestic help as "one of the family," is herself not a highly-educated woman, the "lady-help" too frequently assumes a condescending attitude towards her employer, and the connection naturally proves unsatisfactory. In the second place, a "young lady" from England often hardly understands what hard work really means, and she is too apt to feel that she ought—in virtue of her education—to be excused from various necessary household duties. But if a girl intends to take a "home-help's" position in Canada she should make up her mind not to think any task beneath her dignity which some woman of the house must do. No one really wants a "lady-help" for an ornament, though a lonely woman here and there may desire to have one partly for the sake of companionship. When, indeed, the "help" really makes it her business to "help," the relationship may be very satisfactory; and when she has proved both her usefulness and her refinement she will usually be able to get a situation which ought to satisfy her. Often, however, this will be where the mistress is elderly, or invalided or widowed, for there is not much demand for this kind of assistance in families consisting largely of lively young people. If a lady desires a position as "home-help," I believe it would be well for her to obtain introductions, if possible, to ladies in the province where she is going, as friends often know of each other's needs in such a case, and will gladly assist in bringing the would-be "help" and prospective employer together.

There is a generally good though rather intermittent demand for charwomen and occasional helpers in towns, cities, and the settled rural districts; and the wife of a man who has obtained employment on a farm may often add considerably to the family resources by washing and doing other work for the farmer's wife or neighbours. The wages in the East range from about $1 (4*s.*) a day in the country, to $1·25 (5*s.*), always with meals, in the cities. Some little time ago an enterprising party of young Scotch women, who had come to Toronto to be ordinary servants, clubbed together, took a room or two, and went out working by the day, with the result that they earned more money and had their evenings and Sundays to themselves. They had no difficulty in obtaining as much work as they desired; and their experiment points towards one probable solution of the domestic help problem; but, of course, there are great risks for unprotected girls in every city; and in most Canadian cities the rent of rooms and the cost of living is very high.

Apart from housework, in any form, immense numbers of immigrant girls find employment in shops and factories, and not a few as typists. In Toronto, a typist coming out through the colonization department gets an initial wage of $10 (£2) a week, and one who is also a stenographer gets from $11 (£2 4*s.*) to $15 (£3) the week. In Winnipeg (where there are said to be "ten thousand lady stenographers and book-keepers") "the wages run from $35 (£7) to $75 (£15), or even $100 (£20) per month." The saleswomen in shops do not receive nearly so much, and good wages are very necessary in the towns if a girl is to live under proper and healthful conditions. Women's work is not as yet much organized in Canada, though in Montreal and other cities there are a few women's labour unions.

There is perhaps nearly as much demand for competent dressmakers as for domestic servants, either to make dresses at home or to go out by the day. This demand comes not only from the cities, such as Toronto, where, for example, good dressmakers can earn, in addition to their meals, from $1·50 to $2 (6*s.* to 8*s.*) the day, or Winnipeg, where their charge is $2 or $2·50 (8*s.* to 10*s.*) the day; but from country towns and rural districts. In the latter they can earn $1 or $1·25 (4*s.* to 5*s.*), with board and lodging, for the time of their engagement; and I think it would be well worth while for girls who understand dressmaking to try their fortune in some village in a good farming country. I know that there is a large demand for their services in such places, and though they would not receive city prices for their work, neither would they have to pay city prices for the rooms which they would need as headquarters. In a good village two sisters or friends might very well make the experiment together; or a girl understanding dressmaking, whose parents were coming to the country, might easily work up a good business connection. I should not forget to say that the farmers' wives are quite willing to send a "buggy" or carriage a considerable distance for the dressmaker.

There is a great demand in Canada for teachers, and a father who comes out with a family of young people might well endeavour to get some of them (if they show any aptitude for the work) trained for teachers. It is desirable that the students should finish their preparation and pass the necessary examinations in the province where they intend to teach, as professional teachers' certificates only hold good in the province where they are granted, though temporary "permits" to teach may be given in other provinces.

The rate of salaries varies somewhat in different parts of the Dominion, the salaries given in the West being generally higher than those in the East. There are not many openings for private governesses, though a few find employment in ladies' schools, and there is a small demand in the households of the rich for nursery governesses for very little children.

Girls coming out with the intention of entering any occupation (except that of domestic servants) should have a little money in hand to support them whilst looking for employment; but for women, as for men, there are numerous opportunities in Canada for the alert, intelligent girl—"on the spot"—who knows how to work.

With regard to the acquirement of land, opportunities in Canada are by no means as favourable for women as for men. In a general way women can only obtain land by purchase, and are shut out from the advantage of homesteading; but, as already mentioned, they are permitted in British Columbia to take up pre-emptions on practically the same terms as men. The laws, by the way, concerning the civil rights of women vary in different provinces; but from the women's point of view Canada lags behind some of the States of the Union, in the fact that not one of the nine provinces of the Dominion has, as yet, accorded parliamentary representation to women. Even the people most strongly averse from the change are, however, beginning to prophesy dolefully that "it has got to come."

In educational facilities, the women of Canada are treated liberally. In the public and high schools co-education is general, and usually the universities admit women on the same terms as men. The medical profession is open to women; and in some provinces that of the law also. There are many women journalists and writers who are banded together into an organization for the Dominion—"The Canadian Women's Press Club."

A very active and comprehensive organization in Canada is the "National Council of Women," with which many other women's associations are affiliated. Among these may be named the Women's Institutes (which, in Ontario alone, have over twenty thousand members), the Women's Art Association, the Girls' Friendly Society, the Victorian Order of Nurses, the Canadian Suffrage Association, the National Historical Society, the Peace and Arbitrations Society, etc., etc. There are many other extremely important women's organizations, such as the Missionary Societies (called by different names) of the several churches, which, besides supporting foreign missions, make an especial effort to aid religious work in the newer sections of the Dominion. There is also the Women's Christian Temperance Union, which has for long been engaged in effective work against the liquor traffic.

It may be asked what has all this to do with "the woman Canada needs," and with opportunities for women? My answer is that such a list (which might be much lengthened) shows what the women of Canada are thinking about and working for; that what has been done, may be done again; what is being done now, may be multiplied enormously with the advent of more workers. That these organizations are flourishing suggests the need and the opportunity there is for the work of public-spirited, true-hearted women in Canada—in helping to refine the rough, to smooth down the rugged, to hold up the higher ideals of life in this new land; to fill its towns with pleasant, beautiful homes, and to make its solitary places blossom like the rose.

Canada has scope for the employment of the energies of all of the best types of women, and we have got beyond the notion that there is only one noble type of woman; but if one goes back to that severely practical document, the Census Report, it really looks as if the woman which Canada needs above all is the wife and mother, who is awaiting in the Old Land the chance to rejoin her immigrant husband; and the "marriageable girl." "The Imperial Home Reunion Associations" already mentioned are doing good work in bringing out the former, with her children; but it is a more delicate matter to settle the latter in regions where her best opportunity lies. In the early French times, the authorities managed this matter with business-like frankness, shipping out consignments of girls and marrying them in haste on their arrival in the colony. Such a method is distinctly out-of-date, but more might be done to encourage the immigration of families and of young women (under proper conditions and safeguards), for in the West especially, behind the opportunities for girls as workers in household service and shops and factories and offices, many of them find the opportunity of taking up the *rôle* of the wife, the mother and the "home-maker."

Unfortunately it is a common assertion, that a considerable proportion of girls "in business" are so occupied with the probabilities of "having homes" of their own, that they regard their work at the typewriter or in the office as a mere stopgap, to be performed perfunctorily. Let us hope this is a slander; and at any rate some business men testify that the girl clerk is, as a rule, quite as conscientious, steady-going and dependable as the boy clerk, if not more so. However that may be, the fact remains that there is a need for the coming out to Canada of a good type of girls, more in proportion than at present to the numbers of the male immigrants, if the Dominion is to be, in accord with the best Anglo-Saxon ideals, a nation of homes.

XVIII

HINTS AND SUGGESTIONS

IN the foregoing pages, I have tried not to be led by my real belief in the country into over-statement of the advantages of Canada and to under-statement of difficulties and disadvantages. I know that when all possible care is taken, it is difficult to convey to anyone exact impressions of an unknown country, for the reader or listener naturally translates what is said in terms of his own experience. Now I should like here, before bidding farewell to any reader who has some notion of making a home in Canada, to add one or two suggestions which may save him (or her) some discomfort.

The first is an awkward matter to mention, but I will venture to speak plainly, only reminding the reader that if my remarks are offensive, Canada cannot be held responsible for them, for I am myself an Englishwoman.

I have said, and I firmly believe, that the immigration of people from the British Isles is much desired in Canada; but an individual may not always get that impression, and I should like to ask him to consider whether it may not sometimes be his own fault? It is, unfortunately, a fact that many new arrivals from England (by no means all, of course) have a way of stroking the Canadians the wrong way, if one may use the phrase. Sometimes I wonder whether the phrase in our old school books—the "British Possessions"—has anything to do with the condescending frame of mind in which many a British immigrant lands in the Dominion, and begins cheerfully setting affairs right on his first walk through the seaport town which receives him. Again and again it has been a fine thing in British history that the English people have a way of identifying themselves with their national institutions, but if a Briton will persist on feeling, and making it known, that he is a kind of pocket edition of all that the great British Empire stands for, while the Dominion is "one of our colonies," and the Canadians are just "colonists," he will probably get into trouble in a week with the men whom he undertakes to work for or amongst. He ought to try to realize that, in the main, Canadians are Britons like himself, and that, being "chips of the old block," colonists have many characteristics in common with the stay-at-home Britons—amongst them, a rooted objection to a treatment which seems to imply that they are a nation of inferiors.

Perhaps there is something in the invigorating air of this young country which gets into the heads of newcomers, and makes them "apt to teach" if they never were so in their lives before; but many an immigrant would find his first few months here much smoother, if he could resist the temptation to put into words his wonder "at the way they do things here. Why, in England— —" etc., etc. Of course, if he is an intelligent man, he has his contribution to make to the common stock of knowledge and wisdom, and the time may come when it will be welcome in Canada. In many instances, however, the newcomer does not wait to ascertain whether or not there may be a sound reason, in some peculiarity of climate or circumstances, to account for the practice he condemns, but at once jumps to the conclusion that it is un-English and therefore wrong, and proclaims aloud his discovery at the top of his voice. The "canny Scot" is much less prone to hasty, outspoken criticism, and consequently settles down a little more easily than do Englishmen of a certain type.

It may be said that this blunder on the part of English people is so rare and so limited to the wholly uneducated as to be unworthy of serious attention. But I believe it is common. I know I have heard Englishmen criticizing the shortcomings of "the Canadians" in Canadian houses, where they were guests, with a freedom that accounts for a good deal of prejudice against the new arrivals. Others perpetually grumble during their first months in the country.

Happily this kind of thing soon wears off in all but the very worst subjects, and those usually end by returning home, and continuing their criticism of matters Canadian where they cannot be easily answered. Happily, also, some English immigrants, blessed with a little imagination and the sympathetic power of seeing how things will affect other minds, are free from the disease. It has been suggested that a good and practical rule for an Englishman would be to make up his mind to refrain, for at least a year after his landing, from criticism of the things in Canada that displease him, whether these happen to be manners or methods, municipal regulations or country roads.

Later, when he has got his bearings, if he chooses to attempt to lead a reformation, he will find plenty of native-born Canadians to back him; for, however it may appear in the heat of argument, in nine cases out of ten, they are just as convinced as the newcomer that neither the country nor themselves are anywhere within sight of perfection. In twelve months he may be beginning to feel that he has some part and lot in the Dominion, and the honest criticism of one who is anxious to improve conditions which he has tested and believes to be capable of improvement is a very different matter from the superior and comprehensive grumblings either of "a fish out of water," or a mere "bird of passage." For convenience I have used the masculine pronoun, but the woman-immigrant is not free from this sin of rash and ill-mannered criticism.

Now, in all this I would by no means be understood to be reflecting on the newcomer, who, having suffered from failure on the part of some official or private person to carry out his engagements, or having other real cause of complaint concerning the way in which he has been treated, demands an investigation into his grievance. Of course, the new arrival has his rights as much as the native-born, and if he is at any time ill-used or treated with serious neglect, he will be doing a public service in calling attention to the wrong-doing. This is very different from the mere purposeless grumbling and captious criticism to which I referred above; and while the Dominion and Provincial governments do their utmost to protect the newcomer against misrepresentation and fraud and extortion, there are persons in Canada, as elsewhere, on the watch to take advantage of the inexperienced.

PAUL, A BLACKFOOT INDIAN.

It is best for the immigrant who is without friends in the country to go in the first place for information and advice to the accredited immigration officials. (See Appendix, Note A, pg. 159.) There are different methods in vogue in the different provinces, but all endeavour to look to some extent after the immigrants, who, indeed, are regarded as of great potential value to the nation; and far-sighted people recognize that every measure which aids the immigrant to succeed is of advantage to the public generally, and is a necessary corollary of the fact that the Canadian government maintains fifteen hundred agents in the towns and villages of Great Britain and Ireland, and pays a bonus on each of the immigrants obtained, of certain classes.

In Nova Scotia, in order to prevent newcomers being drawn into the purchase of "farm properties unsuitable to their requirements," a farm inspector has been appointed to the staff of the Bureau of Industries and Immigration, which has been in existence since 1907, and any *bonâ fide* settler can avail himself of his services free of cost. An agricultural settler is met on his arrival, and a list of available farms likely to suit him is prepared for him, and, after he has seen them, but before he buys, the farm inspector visits the property and gives him "a disinterested opinion on the intrinsic value of the place." This plan has been found to work well, insuring for the newcomer good value for his money, and saving him much time and expense in the search for a suitable farm. Moreover, if the new arrival desires it, the inspector will continue his visits at intervals to give expert advice respecting the best local markets and the methods of agriculture best adapted to the land purchased.

In a great many central places, the Dominion government has built Immigration Halls, where free accommodation is provided during two or three days, while the head of the family makes arrangements to go to work or to a homestead, as the case may be; but the immigrants are required to provide their own food. In Toronto, the "British Welcome League" also provides beds for British immigrants on their arrival, and in addition gives a free meal, besides trying in other ways to make the strangers feel at home. (See Appendix, Note F, pg. 163.)

Young women and girls coming to Canada need especially to be on their guard against persons of both sexes, masquerading as benevolent and disinterested, who are seeking to entrap the unwary into the terrible life of the "white slave." If ever at a loss where to go, they should accept advice only from uniformed officers of the Immigration Department, from one of the deaconesses or ladies wearing the "Travellers' Aid" badge, or from an officer of the Salvation Army, which also looks after immigrants. A safe place to make inquiry for lodgings and employment is, of course, any branch of the Young Women's Christian Association, of which there are many in the Dominion. (See Appendix, Note F, pg. 163, for list.) In summer, a secretary of the Y.W.C.A. meets the steamers at Quebec, and will do her best to help girls on their way.

The Presbyterians, the Methodists and the Church of England in Canada have chaplains who meet the immigrant ships at the ports of Halifax and St. John in winter, and at Quebec in summer. There are also agents of the Y.M.C.A. at these ports to assist newcomers in every way possible. If the immigrant can find time on landing to speak either to a chaplain or to an agent of one of the societies named above, it may prove very helpful in finding friends in the place to which he or she is going, for these secretaries will give addresses of clergymen or others anxious to befriend the newcomer; and it is a great advantage to have someone to refer to in a strange place, even if it is only for the sake of being able to obtain disinterested and reliable information. For instance, suppose a girl comes out intending to try dressmaking in a country place (as suggested previously), if she has a card of introduction to a Y.W.C.A. secretary or to a minister, though they might not be able to tell her offhand of a district where she could hope to be successful, either would certainly be able to put her into communication with another secretary, or clergyman's wife, or secretary of a Woman's Institute, who would give the information needed.

It is a good thing for the immigrant who has at home belonged to a church, or Sunday school, or social organization, to bring from the clergyman or minister or teacher a letter of introduction to a minister in the place to which he or she is bound, or to someone living in the district. To give an actual, though perhaps unnecessary, instance of the usefulness of letters of introduction—my father, who, though quite inexperienced in agriculture, had decided to farm in Canada, came out armed with letters of introduction, kindly given by friends (some of whom had hazy ideas of the size of the Dominion) to persons living anywhere from the Atlantic to the Pacific. Many of these were, of course, useless, but one led to another introduction to two excellent Scotch farmers, who, when the time came to make choice of a farm, kindly did for us the work which the Government expert now does for immigrants going to Nova Scotia. They looked over the farm and gave a careful opinion as to its value. No newcomer, however anxious to be independent, however unwilling to "impose upon good nature," need be afraid or ashamed to ask advice in matters where he cannot be supposed to be on a par with those who have had experience of the country.

Years ago it was sometimes suggested that Canada was a good country for persons of small fixed incomes. I doubt whether many of this class ever did come; and now, at any rate, the cost of living and the wages of servants are so high that it is not a good country for such people. Moreover, unless they should come out with their families, elderly men or women would rarely be wise to risk the change of climate and environment.

In this connection, it is very satisfactory that such a large proportion of the children sent out by the various orphanages and "homes" of the British Isles grow up good citizens of the Dominion. Only a very small proportion of these children turn out criminals or ne'er-do-wells, but the rare cases when any of them are convicted of crime are usually followed by a great outcry against bringing them. There is, however, a very practical evidence that they are most welcome, for five to ten applications are received for every child to be placed. There is an advantage in sending them out in early life, for "the sooner they get into the Canadian atmosphere the better it is for Canada and for them." Many of the children fill useful positions, as they grow old enough, as "hired" boys and girls; and not a few are adopted, and well provided for, by childless people. The annual report of the "Chief

Inspector of British Immigrant Children and Receiving and Distributing Homes" is a most interesting document. During the eleven years from 1900 to 1911, nearly twenty-four thousand child-immigrants were brought to Canada by various societies and agents, of whom almost half were from Dr. Barnardo's homes.

The immigration of families consisting of parents and children is still more satisfactory from the Canadian point of view, for this, in ordinary cases, means that the children, brought up under normal conditions, will be assimilating in their early years Canadian customs, methods of work, and habits of thought. This is a process that all immigrants, young or old, must go through to a certain extent, if they are really to "settle" in the country. Speaking broadly, adaptation to new conditions is much more difficult for the young man than for the child, and for the old person than the young, unless in the case of those exceptional people who seem to have discovered the secret of perpetual youth, and are alert, ready to learn, adaptable, and intensely interested in life and their surroundings to old age.

In many instances the process is not only difficult but painful; and I should like to speak a word of encouragement to the immigrant in his first year or two, when the exciting novelty of the change has worn off, and he has not yet become thoroughly acclimatized either to the physical or mental atmosphere of the new country. In some cases he passes through a period of miserable homesickness, when everything seems disappointing. Then, even such minor ills as unfamiliar kinds of implements to work with (for instance, in the case of a woman, stoves in place of the accustomed open fires) seem to add sorely to the hardships of life. I can remember very well the general depression of spirits in our family when we were trying in vain to keep ourselves warm and to cook in bitter wintry weather with green basswood, foisted upon us by our next-door neighbour, who in some other little ways showed himself very ready to "turn an honest (?) penny" out of our inexperience.

But discouragement passes; soon the newcomer learns how to take care of himself, and, looking back, wonders how his "mole-hills" ever came to be such mountains. A good stock of patience and some small sense of humour ought to make part of the equipment of every immigrant, for there is nothing like the power of seeing the funny side of things to help one over the minor trials of life, and it is good not to take oneself too seriously.

Nevertheless, an immigrant should not make himself unnecessarily funny in the eyes of others. For example, unless the young Englishman is bound for the backwoods, it really is not necessary for him to attire himself in the strange and shaggy garments which the town-bred English tailor thinks appropriate for "the colonies." In most towns and settled country districts he will need much the same kind of clothing as he would use in such places in England. Often, during the first winter, the Englishman does not feel the need of much warmer clothing than he was accustomed to wear at home; but he should have a good heavy overcoat, and, if he is bound for the West, a fur coat or one lined with sheepskin will be a great comfort. He should also have a warm cap which he can pull down over his ears when driving, for the ears are peculiarly liable to get frost-bitten, and one or two stout pairs of woollen or warmly-lined leather gloves will be found useful, for here men do not work in the winter months with uncovered hands, except perhaps west of the Rocky Mountains. In the case of a family, every member of it, from the father to the little tots, should be provided with woollen gloves or mittens, warm caps or hoods, and warm underclothing. All these things, and some wraps and rugs in addition, may prove very useful on the voyage at any time of year; and they will usually be needed on the first arrival in Canada, for most immigrants come in the early spring, when the weather is still cold.

Ordinarily, the trains are sufficiently heated, but there is often a good deal of waiting at wharves or stations. There may be a long drive from the railway to the final destination, and it is best to be well provided for such contingencies. Soon after the arrival of the spring immigrant, however, cool, light clothing for the hot months of the Canadian summer will be required, and it is well for a woman to bring, if possible, some supply of cotton blouses and dresses. The woven, porous kind of cotton underclothing is cheap and suitable for the climate. In their first year, Englishwomen often make the mistake of overloading themselves and their children with heavy garments. I remember, on a hot July day, seeing a poor little English year-old baby swathed in one layer of flannel above another, with the perspiration running down its face, while its sisters, old enough, I suppose, to rebel at such treatment, looked comparatively cool and comfortable in light cotton dresses.

Upon the whole, clothing is dearer in Canada than in England, but the extra cost of the various articles is in a measure neutralized by the fact that a cheaper class of goods—that is, cotton and muslin—can be worn, at least in the inland parts, for a longer period in the year. If possible, it is well to bring out a good supply of boots and shoes and clothing, but not too many of such outer garments, which a change of fashion may render conspicuously out-of-date within a year or two, for Canadians of all classes pay a good deal of attention to dress.

It is good to bring some blankets, and wadded quilts and table-linen, which are all more expensive in Canada than in the "Old Country." On the other hand, it is not well for the newcomer of little capital to put too much of his small stock of money into such provision for the future, for often the articles bought far in advance do not seem quite what would be bought after some experience in the new home; and it is most desirable to keep a few pounds—or dollars—on hand against a possible emergency.

In fact, the government requires that every adult immigrant—except farm labourers and domestic servants—should have some money in his or her possession when landing (See Appendix, Note C, pg. 161); and half as much is required for children under eighteen. This rule is strictly kept, and during the last ten years no less than 1,471 immigrants (of course, by no means all British) were sent back on their arrival on account of lack of funds; and a considerable number of British and other immigrants are not allowed to land, or are deported within two years, on account of insanity, tuberculosis, or other diseases of mind or body. Others have been rejected on account of criminality or bad character; or because there was reason to believe that they would be, or had actually become, public charges.

With regard to the question of admittance, it is most desirable that anyone thinking of coming to Canada, and having a suspicion of some defect or disease in himself or any member of his family, should be very careful to make sure before starting whether or not he and the rest of his party would be admitted. In case of doubt, he would be wise to write to the Assistant Superintendent of Emigration, 11 and 12, Charing Cross, London, giving full particulars, for it is worse than useless for anyone to have the trouble and expenses of the sea voyage only to be sent back. It is much better not to start at all.

For information concerning the cost of passage, the amount of baggage allowed, and so forth. (See Appendix, Notes D, pg. 162 and E, pg. 162.)

Where distances are so great as in Canada, it is often necessary for the immigrants to pass several nights on the train. There are three classes of sleeping cars in use on the Canadian railways. In the "colonist sleeping cars," which are free to second-class passengers on the Canadian lines, berths are provided, but they are not upholstered, and the occupants may use such bedding and rugs as they have with them, or the whole outfit of mattress, pillow, blanket, and a pair of curtains can be purchased for the sum of $2·90 (about 12*s*.), or the separate articles in proportion.

When it can be afforded, however, the immigrant would be wise to pay the additional price for a berth in a "tourist sleeper" (which is about half that of the "standard sleepers"). In the tourist cars the accommodation is excellent, bedding is provided, and each car has its attendant porter. The travellers in these cars may either take their meals on the dining-car (when there is one on the train, and when the question of minor expense is not a very important one), or may carry their food with them, making tea for themselves, heating food for a baby, etc., in a little kitchen at the end of the car. These cars are much used, for the sake of convenience, by persons travelling with children who could well afford to travel in the first-class sleepers.

Before buying tickets for Canada, however, the intending emigrant might do well to write to Commissioner D. C. Lamb, of the Salvation Army, which makes arrangements for emigrants (of whom it is said less than 20 per cent. belong to the Army) to obtain tickets from England to certain points in Canada, "including the cost of bed and food on rail." (See Appendix, Note D, pg. 162.) The Army also arranges for "reserved carriages and special rail accommodation, chiefly for women," who "are accompanied by experienced conductresses from the beginning to the end of their journey." (See Appendix, Note F, pg. 163.)

We will now suppose our British immigrant to have reached his destination, in East or West or Central Canada; and our final word to him, perhaps, should be not to be in too much hurry to commit himself to some irrevocable step. If he has capital, it is often wise for him to let it lie for a little while at interest while he gets to know the country, possibly working on wages for someone else. If the newcomer has little money, then it is best to accept for a time almost any honest work that offers, especially work in which something may be learnt of the country; and to change to something more desirable when the chance comes—as it will come—to the alert and thrifty and industrious. For, after all, the newcomer must learn for himself the things he most needs to know. Many of these things cannot be put into a book, for books must deal largely with generalities, while each immigrant brings his own idiosyncrasies to the problem of fitting into a peculiar environment.

Finally, it is good that the newcomer should realize and remember that "immigration" has two sides to it—that the new country deserves consideration as well as the new arrival, and that this "land of opportunities" only yields its best to the man or woman prepared to give as well as to get.

APPENDIX

NOTE A.—LIST OF DOMINION AND PROVINCIAL OFFICIALS WHO WILL GIVE INFORMATION ABOUT CANADA.

Dominion Agents.

England:

Mr. J. Obed Smith, Assistant Superintendent of Emigration, 11-12, Charing Cross, London, S.W.

Mr. A. F. Jury, 48, Lord Street, Liverpool.

Canadian Government Agent, 139, Corporation Street, Birmingham.

Canadian Government Agent, 81, Queen Street, Exeter.

Mr. L. Burnett, 16, Parliament Street, York.

Scotland:

Mr. J. K. Miller, 107, Hope Street, Glasgow.

Mr. G. G. Archibald, 26, Guild Street, Aberdeen.

Ireland:

Mr. John Webster, 17-19, Victoria Street, Belfast.

Mr. Edward O'Kelly, 44, Dawson Street, Dublin.

Provincial Agents.

For Nova Scotia:

Mr. John Howard, Agent-General for Nova Scotia, 57a, Pall Mall, London, S.W., will also furnish information respecting the province.

When a person arrives in Nova Scotia and wishes to secure farm work, he should apply at once to the Dominion Immigration Agent in Halifax, or to Mr. Arthur S. Barnstead, the Secretary of Industries and Immigration for the province, 197, Hollis Street, Halifax.

For New Brunswick:

Call on or write to Mr. A. Bowder, New Brunswick Representative, 37, Southampton Street, London, W.C.; or to Mr. Jas. Gilchrist, Superintendent of

Immigration, 4, Church Street, St. John, N.B., Canada.

For Prince Edward Island:

Apply to J. E. B. McCready, Publicity Agent, Charlottetown, Prince Edward Island.

For Quebec:

Apply personally or by letter to—

Hon. Dr. Pelletier, Agent-General of the Province of Quebec, 36, Kingsway, London, England.

The Department of Colonization, Mines and Fisheries, Quebec, Canada.

Captain Labelle, Immigration Buildings, Quebec, Canada.

Mr. Emile Marquette, 82, St. Antoine Street, Montreal, Canada.

Mr. J. A. Cook, Secretary, Eastern Townships Associated Boards of Trade, Sherbrooke, Quebec.

For Ontario:

Apply to—

N. B. Colcock, Ontario Government Agent, 163, Strand, London, England.

H. A. Macdonell, Director of Colonization, Parliament Buildings, Toronto, Ontario, Canada.

For Manitoba:

J. Bruce Walker, Commissioner of Immigration, Winnipeg, Manitoba.

For Saskatchewan:

Information may be obtained by writing to the Hon. W. R. Motherwell, Minister of Agriculture, Regina, Saskatchewan.

For Alberta:

Address all inquiries to Chief Publicity Commissioner, Department of Agriculture, Edmonton, Alberta.

For British Columbia:

Address Hon. J. H. Turner, Agent-General for British Columbia, Salisbury House, Finsbury Circus, London, England; or the Bureau of Provincial Information, Victoria, B.C.

No fees are charged by Government Agents.

NOTE B.—SYNOPSIS OF DOMINION LAND REGULATIONS CONCERNING FREE GRANTS, ETC..

Any male over eighteen years old, or a widow who is the sole head of a family, may homestead a quarter-section (one hundred and sixty acres) of available Dominion land in Manitoba, Saskatchewan or Alberta. The applicant must appear in person at the Dominion lands agency or sub-agency for the district. Entry by proxy may be made at any agency on certain conditions by father, mother, son, daughter, brother or sister of intending homesteader.

Duties.—Six months' residence upon and cultivation of at least thirty acres of the land, a proportion of which has to be done in each of three years. A homesteader may live within nine miles of his homestead on a farm of at least eighty acres solely owned and occupied by him or by his father, mother, son, daughter, brother or sister. The erection on the homestead of a house worth $300 (£60).

In certain districts a homesteader in good standing may pre-empt a quarter section alongside his homestead. Price $3 (12*s.* 6*d.*) per acre.

Duties.—Must reside six months in each of six years from date of homestead entry (including the time required to earn homestead patent) and cultivate fifty acres extra. The erection on the homestead or pre-emption of a house worth $300 (£60).

A homesteader who has exhausted his homestead right and cannot obtain a pre-emption may take a purchased homestead in certain districts. Price $3 (12*s.* 6*d.*) per acre.

Duties.—Must reside six months in each of three years, cultivate fifty acres and erect a house worth $300 (£60).

Newly-arrived immigrants will receive at any Dominion lands office in Manitoba, Saskatchewan or Alberta, information as to the lands that are open for entry in that district, and from the officers in charge, free of expense, advice and assistance in securing lands to suit them. Full information respecting the land, timber, coal and mineral laws may be obtained on application to the Superintendent of Immigration, Department of the Interior, Ottawa; or the Commissioner of Immigration, Winnipeg, Manitoba. Dominion land agents can furnish information regarding land in their respective districts only.

NOTE C.—REQUIREMENTS AS TO MONEY IMMIGRANTS MUST HAVE IN POSSESSION ON LANDING.

Between November 1 and February 28, the Canadian Government requires that adult passengers shall have at least $50 (£10) in their possession at time of landing, and $25 (£5) for each person under eighteen, together with necessary transportation, or money equal to cost of transportation, to their destination in Canada. Between March 1 and October 30 the money requirement is $25 (£5) and $12·50 (£2 10*s.*). Exceptions to this are persons going as farm labourers and domestic servants who can prove to Immigration Authorities that they have assured employment. They must also be provided with means to reach destination. Also immigrants, whether male or female, going to reside with a relative who is able and willing to support such immigrant, providing immigrant has the means of reaching the place of residence of such relative:—

1. Wife going to husband.
2. Child going to parent.

3. Brother or sister going to brother.

4. Minor going to married or independent sister.

5. Parent going to son or daughter.

NOTE D.—COST OF PASSAGE AND BAGGAGE ALLOWANCE.

There are no assisted passages except, in some provinces, loans by Government to domestic servants. The steamship fares are: Second class, from £8 to £12; children from one year to twelve years, half fare; infants under twelve months, £1. Third class, £5 to £10; children from one year to twelve years, half fare; infants under twelve months, 10*s*. The fare by rail charged to newcomers is one penny a mile.

Colonists are allowed free on ocean steamers twenty cubic feet of baggage for second cabin, and ten cubic feet third-class. On railways in Canada and the States one hundred and fifty pounds for each adult, and seventy-five pounds for each child's half-fare ticket are carried free, but this applies only to personal effects. No single piece of baggage of over two hundred and fifty pounds will be carried on passenger trains, but must be sent by goods train. This must be done also, at additional charge, in the case of all goods not wearing apparel or personal effects.

If free baggage allowance as above is exceeded, the extra charge on steamship will be 9*d.* per cubic foot, second cabin; and 6*d.* per cubic foot, third-class. On the railways the extra charge will be 12 per cent. of the colonist fare for each one hundred pounds or part thereof.

Salvation Army Tickets Covering Cost of Bed and Food on Rail at Inclusive Rates.

To Vancouver, for British Columbia, £17 15*s*.; to Calgary, £15; to Medicine Hat, £14 10*s*.; to Regina, £13 10*s*.; to Winnipeg, for Manitoba, Alberta, and Saskatchewan, £12 5*s*.; to Toronto, for Ontario (10*s*. less from Southampton), £9 5*s*. The figures quoted cover third-class accommodation on the ocean and colonist railway car in Canada. Passengers travelling second-class on the ship can add the extra.

For particulars apply to Commissioner D. C. Lamb, 122, Queen Victoria Street, London, E.C.; or any of the following branch offices: 170A, London Road, Liverpool; 5, Denmark Street, Bristol; 74, Cobourg Street, Plymouth; 203, Hope Street, Glasgow; and 222, Albert Bridge Road, Belfast.

The Army also has a fully-equipped department for dealing with first and second-class business. Address: 122, Queen Victoria Street, London, E.C.

NOTE E.—"SETTLERS' EFFECTS DUTY FREE."

The following is an extract from the Customs tariff of Canada, specifying the articles which can be entered by settlers free of duty:

Item 455. *Settlers' Effects, viz.*:—Wearing apparel, books, usual and reasonable household furniture and other household effects; instruments and tools of trade, occupation or employment, guns, musical instruments, domestic sewing machines, typewriters, bicycles, carts, waggons and other highway vehicles, agricultural implements, and live stock for the farm, not to include live stock or articles for sale, or for use as a contractor's outfit, nor vehicles nor implements moved by mechanical power, nor machinery for use in any manufacturing establishment; all the foregoing if actually owned abroad by the settler for at least six months before his removal to Canada and subject to regulations by the Minister of Customs: Provided that any dutiable articles entered as settlers' effects may not be so entered unless brought by the settler on his first arrival, and shall not be sold or otherwise disposed of without payment of duty until after twelve months' actual use in Canada.

The settler will be required to fill up a form (which will be supplied to him by the Customs officer on application) giving description, value, etc., of the goods and articles he wishes to be allowed to bring in free of duty.

NOTE F.—YOUNG WOMEN'S CHRISTIAN ASSOCIATIONS DIRECTORY, ETC.

Directory of the Young Women's Christian Associations of Canada.

Name. Address.	General Secretary.
Ontario:	
Berlin, 72, Queen St. E.	
Brantford, Victoria Park	Miss Best.
Hamilton, 17, Main St. W.	Miss I. Mackenzie.
Kingston, 196, Johnson St.	Miss L. K. Knowles.
London, 510, Wellington St.	
London, 326, Dundas St.	
Ottawa, 135, Metcalfe St.	Miss C. Sutcliffe.
Peterborough, 230, Simcoe	Mrs. Grey.
Stratford, 45, Waterloo St.	Miss Dand.
St. Thomas, 250, Talbot St.	Miss B. K. Gunn.
Toronto, 18 Elm St.	Miss Pierce.
Toronto, Elm House, 18 Elm St.	
Toronto, Simcoe House, 180, Simcoe St.	
Toronto, Dufferin House, 248, Dufferin St.	
Toronto, Pembroke House, 76, Pembroke St.	
Toronto, Alexandra House, 240, St. Patrick St.	

Toronto, Ontario House, 698, Ontario St.	
Toronto, Club Rooms, 1684, Dundas St.	Miss Steinhoff.
Toronto, Educational Building, 21, McGill St.	Miss A. Peacock, Educational Secretary.
Quebec:	
Montreal, 502, Dorchester St. W.	
Montreal, Montreal Branch, 39, McGill Col. Ave.	
Montreal, Montreal Branch, 151, Fairmount Ave.	
Quebec, 125, St. Anne St.	Miss Townsend.
Sherbrooke, 2, Moore St.	
Nova Scotia:	
Halifax, 65, Hollis St.	Miss Harrington.
Manitoba:	
Brandon, 117, Tenth St.	Miss E. McGregor.
Brandon, 148, Eleventh St.	
Winnipeg, Ellice Ave. West	Miss N. Elliott.
Winnipeg, Branches, 35-37, Hargrave St.	
Corner Logan and Martha Streets.	
Saskatchewan:	
Moose Jaw, 26, Ominica St.	Miss W. Marlatt.
Prince Albert, 187, Ninth St.	Miss Medhurst.
Regina, 1950, Lorne Ave.	Miss Morton.
Saskatoon, Third Ave. and Twenty-fourth St.	Miss Tuckey.
Alberta:	
Calgary, 223, 12th Ave. W.	Miss Glass.
Edmonton, 526, Third St.	Miss Lukes.
First Avenue, South.	
British Columbia:	
Vancouver, 997, Dunsmuir St.	Miss M. O. Anderson.
Vancouver, Branches, 1017, Dunsmuir St.; 1008, Eveleigh St.; 832, Pender St. E.	

Victoria, 1904, Quadra St. | Miss Bradshaw.

A Secretary will meet all steamers at Quebec, and will be glad to render assistance to those arriving.

In many of the large city depôts there is a Traveller's Aid Secretary, whom it is wise to consult if desirous of any information.

Young women coming as strangers are urged not to seek advice from any but uniformed officers, deaconesses and Traveller's Aid Secretaries.

The Young Women's Christian Association is a recognised centre where any young woman may go for advice.

Salvation Army Hostels for Women-Immigrants.—Cathcart Lodge, 24, Cathcart Street, Montreal; Rosedale Lodge, 916, Yonge Street, Toronto; Balmoral Lodge, Mountain Avenue, Winnipeg; and Pleasant Lodge, 75, Seventh Avenue East, Vancouver.

Women Domestics.

The Salvation Army Emigration Department undertakes:

1. To advance, if necessary, by way of loan, part of the passage money to approved domestic servants.

2. To give free and disinterested advice as to the best locality in which to settle and the best time to go.

3. To safely take parties of girls to Canada under the care of experienced conductors.

4. To have parties of girls met by our own officers on arrival in Canada, conducted through the Customs and to the trains, and thence to their destinations.

5. To guarantee employment before leaving England to all domestic servants emigrating to Canada under our auspices.

6. To accommodate girls in one of our four Hostels in Canada, should it be necessary to wait a day or two before going to their situations.

British Welcome League (for Men, Women and Children), 4 Spadina Avenue, Toronto.

Young Men's Christian Association (Dominion Headquarters),15, Toronto Street, Toronto.

Imperial Home Reunion Association.

Winnipeg Offices: The Winnipeg Industrial Bureau, Main and Water Streets ('Phone M 1,000). (Interest at the rate of 6 per cent. per annum charged on all loans.) Branches at Winnipeg, Toronto, Montreal, Vancouver, Edmonton, Calgary, Hamilton, Brandon, Ottawa, Regina, Red Deer, Moose Jaw, Yorkton, St. John, Medicine Hat, Halifax, Nelson, Gait, Weyburn, Dauphin, Victoria, Fort William, Lethbridge, London, Peterborough.

NOTE G.— BRITISH EQUIVALENT OF CANADIAN MONEY.

		s.	*d.*
5	cents (known as a "nickel")		2½
10	cents (known as a "dime")		5
25	cents (known as a "quarter")	1	0½

1 dollar = 4*s.* 2*d.*

An English sovereign is worth $4·86.

INDEX

D

E

F

L

M

N

O

P

Q

R

V

W

Y

Lector House believes that a society develops through a two-fold approach of continuous learning and adaptation, which is derived from the study of classic literary works spread across the historic timeline of literature records. Therefore, we aim at reviving, repairing and redeveloping all those inaccessible or damaged but historically as well as culturally important literature across subjects so that the future generations may have an opportunity to study and learn from past works to embark upon a journey of creating a better future.

This book is a result of an effort made by Lector House towards making a contribution to the preservation and repair of original ancient works which might hold historical significance to the approach of continuous learning across subjects.

HAPPY READING & LEARNING!

LECTOR HOUSE LLP
E-MAIL: info@lectorhouse.com

9 789356 146013

Printed by Libri Plureos GmbH in Hamburg,
Germany